Gender

Other Books in the Issues on Trial Series:

Gender

Noël Merino, Book Editor

GREENHAVEN PRESS
A part of Gale, Cengage Learning

Detroit • New York • San Francisco • New Haven, Conn • Waterville, Maine • London

Christine Nasso, *Publisher*
Elizabeth Des Chenes, *Managing Editor*

© 2011 Greenhaven Press, a part of Gale, Cengage Learning

For more information, contact:
Greenhaven Press
27500 Drake Rd.
Farmington Hills, MI 48331-3535
Or you can visit our Internet site at gale.cengage.com.

For product information and technology assistance, contact us at

Gale Customer Support, 1-800-877-4253
For permission to use material from this text or product, submit all requests online at www.cengage.com/permissions

Further permissions questions can be emailed to permissionrequest@cengage.com

Articles in Greenhaven Press anthologies are often edited for length to meet page requirements. In addition, original titles of these works are changed to clearly present the main thesis and to explicitly indicate the author's opinion. Every effort is made to ensure that Greenhaven Press accurately reflects the original intent of the authors. Every effort has been made to trace the owners of copyrighted material.

Cover Image © Jim West/Alamy.

LIBRARY OF CONGRESS CATALOGING-IN-PUBLICATION DATA

Gender / Noël Merino, book editor.
    p. cm. -- (Issues on trial)
    Includes bibliographical references and index.
    ISBN 978-0-7377-4948-9 (hardcover)
    1. Sex discrimination against women--Law and legislation--United States. 2. Sex discrimination against women--Law and legislation--United States--Cases. 3. Sex discrimination--United States. I. Merino, Noël.
    KF4758.G46 2010
    342.7308'7--dc22

                                                                    2010020230

Printed in the United States of America
1 2 3 4 5 6 7 14 13 12 11 10

Contents

A law professor argues that the judicial deference to military policy shown in *Rotsker* is outdated and dangerous.

Chapter 2: Employment Decisions Influenced by Gender Stereotypes Are Discriminatory

Chapter 3: Finding Virginia Military Institute's Single-Sex Policy Unconstitutional

An attorney argues that the appeals court's finding in *Smith* went too far in allowing claims of discrimination based on nonstereotypical behavior.

Foreword

The U.S. courts have long served as a battleground for the most highly charged and contentious issues of the time. Divisive matters are often brought into the legal system by activists who feel strongly for their cause and demand an official resolution. Indeed, subjects that give rise to intense emotions or involve closely held religious or moral beliefs lay at the heart of the most polemical court rulings in history. One such case was *Brown v. Board of Education* (1954), which ended racial segregation in schools. Prior to *Brown*, the courts had held that blacks could be forced to use separate facilities as long as these facilities were equal to that of whites.

For years many groups had opposed segregation based on religious, moral, and legal grounds. Educators produced heartfelt testimony that segregated schooling greatly disadvantaged black children. They noted that in comparison to whites, blacks received a substandard education in deplorable conditions. Religious leaders such as Martin Luther King Jr. preached that the harsh treatment of blacks was immoral and unjust. Many involved in civil rights law, such as Thurgood Marshall, called for equal protection of all people under the law, as their study of the Constitution had indicated that segregation was illegal and un-American. Whatever their motivation for ending the practice, and despite the threats they received from segregationists, these ardent activists remained unwavering in their cause.

Those fighting against the integration of schools were mainly white southerners who did not believe that whites and blacks should intermingle. Blacks were subordinate to whites, they maintained, and society had to resist any attempt to break down strict color lines. Some white southerners charged that segregated schooling was *not* hindering blacks' education. For example, Virginia attorney general J. Lindsay Almond asserted, "With the help and the sympathy and the love and re-spect of the white people of the South, the colored man has risen under that educational process to a place of eminence and respect throughout the nation. It has served him well." So when the Supreme Court ruled against the segregationists in *Brown*, the South responded with vociferous cries of protest. Even government leaders criticized the decision. The governor of Arkansas, Orval Faubus, stated that he would not "be a party to any attempt to force acceptance of change to which the people are so overwhelmingly opposed." Indeed, resistance to integration was so great that when black students arrived at the formerly all-white Central High School in Arkansas, fed-eral troops had to be dispatched to quell a threatening mob of protesters.

Nevertheless, the *Brown* decision was enforced and the South integrated its schools. In this instance, the Court, while not settling the issue to everyone's satisfaction, functioned as an instrument of progress by forcing a major social change. Historian David Halberstam observes that the *Brown* ruling "deprived segregationist practices of their moral legitimacy. . . . It was therefore perhaps the single most important moment of the decade, the moment that separated the old order from the new and helped create the tumultuous era just arriving." Considered one of the most important victories for civil rights, *Brown* paved the way for challenges to racial segregation in many areas, including on public buses and in restaurants.

In examining *Brown*, it becomes apparent that the courts play an influential role—and face an arduous challenge—in shaping the debate over emotionally charged social issues. Judges must balance competing interests, keeping in mind the high stakes and intense emotions on both sides. As exempli-fied by *Brown*, judicial decisions often upset the status quo and initiate significant changes in society. Greenhaven Press's Issues on Trial series captures the controversy surrounding in-fluential court rulings and explores the social ramifications of such decisions from varying perspectives. Each anthology highlights one social issue—such as the death penalty, students' rights, or wartime civil liberties. Each volume then focuses on key historical and contemporary court cases that helped mold the issue as we know it today. The books include a compendium of primary sources—court rulings, dissents, and immediate reactions to the rulings—as well as secondary sources from experts in the field, people involved in the cases, legal analysts, and other commentators opining on the implications and legacy of the chosen cases. An annotated table of contents, an in-depth introduction, and prefaces that overview each case all provide context as readers delve into the topic at hand. To help students fully probe the subject, each volume contains book and periodical bibliographies, a comprehensive index, and a list of organizations to contact. With these features, the Issues on Trial series offers a well-rounded perspective on the courts' role in framing society's thorniest, most impassioned debates.

Introduction

The courts' evolving understanding of sex discrimination shows how sex and gender have been treated under the law in the past several decades. The terms "gender" and "sex" are often used interchangeably, referring to a person being either male or female. "Sex discrimination" and "gender discrimination" usually refer to discrimination on the basis of being either male or female. More nuanced discussion of the difference between sex and gender in the courts has occurred in recent years as courts deal with cases where discrimination is alleged on the basis of the way one acts versus one's biological sex. In this sense, "gender" is more often used to refer to a person's masculinity or femininity in appearance and behavior, and "sex" is used, in contrast, to designate the physiological characteristics of a person that make them male or female.

Equal Protection

All people have a right to equal protection of the laws under the equal protection clause of the Fourteenth Amendment, which provides that "no state shall . . . deny any person within its jurisdiction the equal protection of the laws." Despite the clause, women have not always been guaranteed the same protection of the laws as men. In the 1873 case of *Bradwell v. Illinois*, the U.S. Supreme Court upheld a state law that denied women the right to practice law because of their supposed "delicacy." Similarly, the Court in *Minor v. Happersett* (1875) refused to assert that the Fourteenth Amendment required states to allow women to vote. This decision was overturned by the adoption of the Nineteenth Amendment to the U.S. Constitution in 1920. Outside of voting, however, the Court continued to uphold many laws treating men and women differently without justification.

This began to change after the passage of the Equal Pay Act of 1963 and the Civil Rights Act of 1964. Title VII of the Civil Rights Act of 1964 makes it "an unlawful employment practice for an employer . . . to discriminate against any individual with respect to his compensation [pay], terms, conditions, or privileges of employment, because of such individual's race, color, religion, sex, or national origin." After the passage of the Civil Rights Act of 1964, women had a law under which they could seek equal protection in the courts, and the courts changed their understanding of the Fourteenth Amendment as it applies to women.

A Shift in Equal Protection

The right to equal protection based on sex became acknowledged as a constitutional mandate under the Fourteenth Amendment's equal protection clause through a series of cases in the 1970s. In *Reed v. Reed* (1971), the Court struck down a state law that gave men automatic preference over women in the administration of the estate of someone who died without a will. The Court's recognition of equal protection regarding sex did not always apply to laws that discriminated against women: In *Frontiero v. Richardson* (1973), it struck down a law that required husbands of military wives—but not wives of military husbands—to prove dependency in order to receive benefits. In *Craig v. Boren* (1976) the Court struck down a sex-specific restriction on beer purchases. It articulated the standard that the Court should use to review gender distinctions in law: whether a statutory gender distinction is "substantially related to important government objectives."

This standard in *Craig* allows a state to treat women differently from men if the state has an important objective in so doing. Hence, laws making distinctions based on sex are not always unconstitutional. In *Rostker v. Goldberg* (1981) the Court upheld the provision of the Military Selective Service Act requiring only men to register for the draft. Similarly, in

Michael M. v. Superior Court of Sonoma County (1981) the Court upheld a statute that specified criminal penalties only for men in statutory rape cases. However, barring an important state objective, the Court has declared unconstitutional laws that it deems as treating men and women differently for no good reason: In *Mississippi University for Women v. Hogan* (1982) the Court struck down a women-only admissions policy at a state university school of nursing, and in *United States v. Virginia* (1996) it struck down a male-only admissions policy at a state military school. In both cases, the Court did not specifically forbid all publicly funded single-sex education but did note in *Virginia* that it demands an "exceedingly persuasive justification."

Title VII Cases

Title VII, as explained above, prohibits employers from discriminating on the basis of sex. This does not mean employers must always treat women and men exactly the same. For instance, in *California Federal Savings and Loan Association v. Guerra* (1987), the Court concluded that a California law requiring employers to offer pregnancy leave was not unconstitutional, even though it could only ever apply to women.

Under Title VII, courts have found many employers liable for sex discrimination by making employment decisions on the basis of sex. An important case in 1989, *Price Waterhouse v. Hopkins*, extended the understanding of sex discrimination to apply not only to unfavorable employment decisions based on a person's sex, but also to unfavorable employment decisions based on sex stereotyping. *Price Waterhouse* changed the legal understanding of sex discrimination by noting that discrimination was sometimes based not precisely on a person's sex, but on expectations about how a person of a certain sex should act—that is, his or her gender. In *Price Waterhouse v. Hopkins*, the Court determined that sex-stereotyping remarks made about a woman during consideration of her promotion constituted sex discrimination.

Most interesting about *Price Waterhouse v. Hopkins* is how the decision may affect transgendered persons, transsexuals, and homosexuals in the future. Several courts below the level of the U.S. Supreme Court have found that Title VII's protections against sex discrimination apply to transgendered persons and transsexuals. This was the decision of the U.S. Court of Appeals for the Sixth District in *Smith v. Salem, Ohio, et al.* (2004). Given the broader understanding of sex stereotyping based on gender articulated by the Court in *Price Waterhouse*, it is likely that courts will continue to grapple with how Title VII applies to transgendered persons and transsexuals. Similarly, in the case of *Prowel v. Wise Business Forms, Inc.* (2009), the United States Third Circuit Court of Appeals held that a homosexual employee who was harassed by coworkers could pursue a claim of "gender stereotyping" under Title VII.

The understanding of sex discrimination in the courts continues to evolve, as does the relevance of sex and gender to this concept. By presenting the court decisions, the views of dissenting justices, and commentary on the impact of cases on the issue of gender, *Issues on Trial: Gender* sheds light on how the legal understanding of gender in the United States has evolved and continues to do so.

CHAPTER 1

Upholding Selective Service Registration for Males Only

Case Overview

Rostker v. Goldberg (1981)

In *Rostker v. Goldberg*, the U.S. Supreme Court upheld the constitutionality of the male-only draft registration law, the Military Selective Service Act (MSSA), enacted by Congress in 1980. The case started in 1971, during the last part of the Vietnam War. Robert Goldberg and several other men challenged the male-only draft policy, arguing that their right to equal protection of the laws, as guaranteed by the Fifth Amendment, had been violated. Congress discontinued military conscription in 1972, but it was revived in 1980 at the request of President Jimmy Carter, due to concern about the Soviet Union's invasion of Afghanistan. Carter proposed the inclusion of women in the draft registration, but Congress rejected his proposal after holding hearings on the issue. Goldberg's lawsuit was reactivated after Carter signed the Military Selective Service Act, which ordered registration of young men only.

A three-judge panel in the U.S. district court held a hearing on Goldberg's claims against Bernard Rostker, director of the Selective Service System, the agency that administers military registration. The panel agreed with Goldberg and the other plantiffs that the law violated equal protection, declaring it unconstitutional three days before registration was to start. Rostker appealed the decision to the U.S. Supreme Court; his request that the court's order be temporarily lifted pending appeal was granted, and registration proceeded.

Justice William Rehnquist wrote the decision for the U.S. Supreme Court, with five other justices joining him. The plaintiffs' claim that the male-only draft restriction violated their guarantee of the equal protection of the laws was rejected by the Court. In considering this claim, Rehnquist noted that Congress had considered the inclusion of women and had decided that it would interfere with the military's goals of establishing combat troops. At the time, there was a prohibition against women serving in combat positions. Military leaders had explained to Congress that commanders would be restricted in their flexibility in the use of military personnel if women were drafted, since women would be restricted to support roles. Rehnquist saw no reason to second-guess Congress' review of this issue and argued that because women were excluded from combat, there was a justification for treating men and women differently with respect to mandatory military registration. The Court concluded that male-only requirement of the MSSA was constitutional.

Three justices dissented from the Court's ruling. Byron White and Thurgood Marshall each filed dissenting opinions, disagreeing with the Court that a complete exclusion of women from draft registration was necessary for the military to achieve its goals. Neither, however, questioned the prohibition against women serving in combat.

Since the Court's decision in *Rostker*, the role of women in combat has changed. Although women are officially prohibited from ground combat, women soldiers have become more closely involved in combat in recent wars. Many argue that the policy prohibiting women in combat is no longer relevant and not followed in many instances. If this policy were to be lifted, it is unclear whether the decision in *Rostker* would be upheld.

"Congress acted well within its constitutional authority when it authorized the registration of men, and not women, under the Military Selective Service Act."

Majority Opinion: The Military Selective Service Act Is Constitutional

William Rehnquist

William Rehnquist was a Supreme Court justice from 1972 to 2005, the last nineteen years of which he served as chief justice. Rehnquist was considered a conservative member of the Court.

The following is the majority opinion in the 1981 case of Rostker v. Goldberg, *the Supreme Court ruling that upheld the constitutionality of the male-only registration requirement of the Military Selective Service Act (MSSA). In this opinion, Rehnquist argues that the judicial branch of government needs to give deference to the legislative branch, Congress, especially when the subject of the legislation is national defense and military affairs. The Court concludes that the district court overstepped its bounds in finding the MSSA in violation of the U.S. Constitution and that there is nothing unconstitutional about Congress's decision to limit mandatory military registration to men.*

The question presented is whether the Military Selective Service Act [MSSA] violates the Fifth Amendment to the United States Constitution in authorizing the President to require the registration of males, and not females. . . .

William Rehnquist, majority opinion, *Rostker v. Goldberg*, U.S. Supreme Court, June 25, 1981.

A Complaint by Male Registrants

On July 2, 1980, the President, by Proclamation, ordered the registration of specified groups of young men pursuant to the authority conferred by § 3 of the Act. Registration was to commence on July 21, 1980.

These events of last year breathed new life into a lawsuit which had been essentially dormant in the lower courts for nearly a decade. It began in 1971, when several men subject to registration for the draft and subsequent induction into the Armed Services filed a complaint in the United States District Court for the Eastern District of Pennsylvania challenging the MSSA on several grounds. A three-judge District Court was convened in 1974 to consider the claim of unlawful gender-based discrimination which is now before us. On July 1, 1974, the court declined to dismiss the case as moot, reasoning that, although authority to induct registrants had lapsed, plaintiffs were still under certain affirmative obligations in connection with registration. Nothing more happened in the case for five years. Then, on June 6, 1979, the court Clerk, acting pursuant to a local rule governing inactive cases, proposed that the case be dismissed. Additional discovery thereupon ensued, and defendants moved to dismiss on various justiciability grounds. The court denied the motion to dismiss, ruling that it did not have before it an adequate record on the operation of the Selective Service System and what action would be necessary to reactivate it. On July 1, 1980, the court certified a plaintiff class of

> all male persons who are registered or subject to registration under 50 U.S.C.App. § 453 or are liable for training and service in the armed forces of the United States under 50 U.S-.C.App. §§ 454, 456 (h) and 467 (c).

The District Court's Decision

On Friday, July 18, 1980, three days before registration was to commence, the District Court issued an opinion finding that the Act violated the Due Process Clause of the Fifth Amendment and permanently enjoined the Government from requiring registration under the Act. The court initially determined that the plaintiffs had standing and that the case was ripe, determinations which are not challenged here by the Government. Turning to the merits, the court rejected plaintiffs' suggestions that the equal protection claim should be tested under "strict scrutiny," and also rejected defendants' argument that the deference due Congress in the area of military affairs required application of the traditional "minimum scrutiny" test. Applying the "important government interest" test articulated in *Craig v. Boren* (1976), the court struck down the MSSA. The court stressed that it was not deciding whether or to what extent women should serve in combat, but only the issue of registration, and felt that this "should dispel any concern that we are injecting ourselves in an inappropriate manner into military affairs." The court then proceeded to examine the testimony and hearing evidence presented to Congress by representatives of the military and the Executive Branch, and concluded on the basis of this testimony that

> military opinion, backed by extensive study, is that the availability of women registrants would materially increase flexibility, not hamper it.

It rejected Congress' contrary determination in part because of what it viewed as Congress' "inconsistent positions" in declining to register women yet spending funds to recruit them and expand their opportunities in the military.

The Director of Selective Service immediately filed a notice of appeal, and the next day, Saturday, July 19, 1980, Justice [William J.] Brennan acting in his capacity as Circuit Justice for the Third Circuit, stayed the District Court's order enjoining commencement of registration. Registration began the next Monday. On December 1, 1980, we noted probable jurisdiction.

Customary Deference to Congress

Whenever called upon to judge the constitutionality of an Act of Congress—"the gravest and most delicate duty that this Court is called upon to perform" [*Blodett v. Holden* (1927)]— the Court accords "great weight to the decisions of Congress" [*Columbia Broadcasting System, Inc. v. Democratic National Committee* (1973)]. The Congress is a coequal branch of government whose Members take the same oath we do to uphold the Constitution of the United States. As Justice [Felix] Frankfurter noted in *Joint Anti-Fascist Refugee Committee v. McGrath* (1951) (concurring opinion), we must have

> due regard to the fact that this Court is not exercising a primary judgment, but is sitting in judgment upon those who also have taken the oath to observe the Constitution and who have the responsibility for carrying on government.

The customary deference accorded the judgments of Congress is certainly appropriate when, as here, Congress specifically considered the question of the Act's constitutionality.

This is not, however, merely a case involving the customary deference accorded congressional decisions. The case arises in the context of Congress' authority over national defense and military affairs, and perhaps in no other area has the Court accorded Congress greater deference. In rejecting the registration of women, Congress explicitly relied upon its constitutional powers under Art. I, § 8, cls. 12–14. The "specific findings" section of the Report of the Senate Armed Services Committee, later adopted by both Houses of Congress, began by stating:

> Article I, section 8 of the Constitution commits exclusively to the Congress the powers to raise and support armies, provide and maintain a Navy, and make rules for Government and regulation of the land and naval forces, and pursuant to these powers it ties within the discretion of the Congress to determine the occasions for expansion of our

Armed Forces, and the means best suited to such expansion, should it prove necessary.

This Court has consistently recognized Congress' "broad constitutional power" to raise and regulate armies and navies [*Schlesinger v. Ballard* (1975)]. As the Court noted in considering a challenge to the selective service laws:

> The constitutional power of Congress to raise and support armies and to make all laws necessary and proper to that end is broad and sweeping. [*United States v. O'Brien* (1968).]

Not only is the scope of Congress' constitutional power in this area broad, but the lack of competence on the part of the courts is marked. In *Gilligan v. Morgan* (1973), the Court noted:

> [I]t is difficult to conceive of an area of governmental activity in which the courts have less competence. The complex, subtle, and professional decisions as to the composition, training, equipping, and control of a military force are essentially professional military judgments, subject always to civilian control of the Legislative and Executive Branches....

The Question for the Court

None of this is to say that Congress is free to disregard the Constitution when it acts in the area of military affairs. In that area, as any other, Congress remains subject to the limitations of the Due Process Clause, but the tests and limitations to be applied may differ because of the military context. We, of course, do not abdicate our ultimate responsibility to decide the constitutional question, but simply recognize that the Constitution itself requires such deference to congressional choice. In deciding the question before us, we must be particularly careful not to substitute our judgment of what is desirable for that of Congress, or our own evaluation of evidence for a reasonable evaluation by the Legislative Branch....

No one could deny that, under the test of *Craig v. Boren*, the Government's interest in raising and supporting armies is an "important governmental interest." Congress and its Committees carefully considered and debated two alternative means of furthering that interest: the first was to register only males for potential conscription, and the other was to register both sexes. Congress chose the former alternative. When that decision is challenged on equal protection grounds, the question a court must decide is not which alternative it would have chosen, had it been the primary decisionmaker, but whether that chosen by Congress denies equal protection of the laws. . . .

Hearings by Congress

This case is quite different from several of the gender-based discrimination cases we have considered in that, despite appellees' assertions, Congress did not act "unthinkingly" or "reflexively and not for any considered reason." The question of registering women for the draft not only received considerable national attention and was the subject of wide-ranging public debate, but also was extensively considered by Congress in hearings, floor debate, and in committee. Hearings held by both Houses of Congress in response to the President's request for authorization to register women adduced extensive testimony and evidence concerning the issue. These hearings built on other hearings held the previous year addressed to the same question.

The House declined to provide for the registration of women when it passed the Joint Resolution allocating funds for the Selective Service System. When the Senate considered the Joint Resolution, it defeated, after extensive debate, an amendment which, in effect, would have authorized the registration of women. . . .

While proposals to register women were being rejected in the course of transferring funds to register males, Committees in both Houses which had conducted hearings on the issue were also rejecting the registration of women. . . .

Congress determined that any future draft, which would be facilitated by the registration scheme, would be characterized by a need for combat troops. The Senate Report explained, in a specific finding later adopted by both Houses, that, "[i]f mobilization were to be ordered in a wartime scenario, the primary manpower need would be for combat replacements." This conclusion echoed one made a year before by the same Senate Committee. As Senator [Roger] Jepsen put it, "the shortage would be in the combat arms. That is why you have drafts." Congress' determination that the need would be for combat troops if a draft took place was sufficiently supported by testimony adduced at the hearings so that the courts are not free to make their own judgment on the question. The purpose of registration, therefore, was to prepare for a draft *of combat troops.*

Women and Combat

Women as a group, however, unlike men as a group, are not eligible for combat. The restrictions on the participation of women in combat in the Navy and Air Force are statutory. Under 10 U.S.C. § 6015, "women may not be assigned to duty on vessels or in aircraft that are engaged in combat missions," and under 10 U.S.C. § 8549 female members of the Air Force "may not be assigned to duty in aircraft engaged in combat missions." The Army and Marine Corps preclude the use of women in combat as a matter of established policy. Congress specifically recognized and endorsed the exclusion of women from combat in exempting women from registration. In the words of the Senate Report:

> The principle that women should not intentionally and routinely engage in combat is fundamental, and enjoys wide support among our people. It is universally supported by military leaders who have testified before the Committee. . . . Current law and policy exclude women from being assigned to combat in our military forces, and the Committee reaffirms this policy.

27

The Senate Report specifically found that "[w]omen should not be intentionally or routinely placed in combat positions in our military services." The President expressed his intent to continue the current military policy precluding women from combat, and appellees present their argument concerning registration against the background of such restrictions on the use of women in combat. Consistent with the approach of this Court in *Schlesinger v. Ballard*, we must examine appellees' constitutional claim concerning registration with these combat restrictions firmly in mind.

The existence of the combat restrictions clearly indicates the basis for Congress' decision to exempt women from registration. The purpose of registration was to prepare for a draft of combat troops. Since women are excluded from combat, Congress concluded that they would not be needed in the event of a draft, and therefore decided not to register them. Again turning to the Senate Report:

> In the Committee's view, the starting point for any discussion of the appropriateness of registering women for the draft is the question of the proper role of women in combat. . . . The policy precluding the use of women in combat is, in the Committee's view, the most important reason for not including women in a registration system.

The Gender Classification

The District Court stressed that the military need for women was irrelevant to the issue of their registration. As that court put it:

> Congress could not constitutionally require registration under the MSSA of only black citizens or only white citizens, or single out any political or religious group simply because those groups contain sufficient persons to fill the needs of the Selective Service System.

This reasoning is beside the point. The reason women are exempt from registration is not because military needs can be met by drafting men. This is not a case of Congress arbitrarily choosing to burden one of two similarly situated groups, such as would be the case with an all-black or all-white, or an all-Catholic or all-Lutheran, or an all-Republican or all-Democratic registration. Men and women, because of the combat restrictions on women, are simply not similarly situated for purposes of a draft or registration for a draft.

Congress' decision to authorize the registration of only men, therefore, does not violate the Due Process Clause. The exemption of women from registration is not only sufficiently, but also closely, related to Congress' purpose in authorizing registration. The fact that Congress and the Executive have decided that women should not serve in combat fully justifies Congress in not authorizing their registration, since the purpose of registration is to develop a pool of potential combat troops. As was the case in *Schlesinger v. Ballard*, "the gender classification is not invidious, but rather realistically reflects the fact that the sexes are not similarly situated" in this case [*Michael M. v. Superior Court of Sonoma County* (1981)]. The Constitution requires that Congress treat similarly situated persons similarly, not that it engage in gestures of superficial equality.

In holding the MSSA constitutionally invalid, the District Court relied heavily on the President's decision to seek authority to register women and the testimony of members of the Executive Branch and the military in support of that decision. As stated by the administration's witnesses before Congress, however, the President's "decision to ask for authority to register women is based on equity." This was also the basis for the testimony by military officials. The Senate Report evaluating the testimony before the Committee, recognized that "[t]he argument for registration and induction of women . . . is not based on military necessity, but on considerations of equity." Congress was certainly entitled, in the exercise of its constitutional powers to raise and regulate armies and navies, to focus on the question of military need rather than "equity." As Senator [Sam] Nunn of the Senate Armed Services Committee put it:

> Our committee went into very great detail. We found that there was no military necessity cited by any witnesses for the registration of females.

> The main point that those who favored the registration of females made was that they were in favor of this because of the equality issue, which is, of course, a legitimate view. But as far as military necessity, and that is what we are primarily, I hope, considering in the overall registration bill, there is no military necessity for this.

Evaluation of the Evidence

Although the military experts who testified in favor of registering women uniformly opposed the actual drafting of women, there was testimony that in the event of a draft of 650,000 the military could absorb some 80,000 female inductees. The 80,000 would be used to fill noncombat positions, freeing men to go to the front. In relying on this testimony in striking down the MSSA, the District Court palpably exceeded its authority when it ignored Congress' considered response to this line of reasoning.

In the first place, assuming that a small number of women could be drafted for noncombat roles, Congress simply did not consider it worth the added burdens of including women in draft and registration plans.

> It has been suggested that all women be registered, but only a handful actually be inducted in an emergency. The Committee finds this a confused and ultimately unsatisfactory solution.

As the Senate Committee recognized a year before, "training would be needlessly burdened by women recruits who could not be used in combat." It is not for this Court to dismiss such problems as insignificant in the context of military preparedness and the exigencies of a future mobilization.

Congress also concluded that whatever the need for women for noncombat roles during mobilization, whether 80,000 or less, it could be met by volunteers.

Most significantly, Congress determined that staffing noncombat positions with women during a mobilization would be positively detrimental to the important goal of military flexibility.

> ... [T]here are other military reasons that preclude very large numbers of women from serving. Military flexibility requires that a commander be able to move units or ships quickly. Units or ships not located at the front or not previously scheduled for the front nevertheless must be able to move into action if necessary. In peace and war, significant rotation of personnel is necessary, we should not divide the military into two groups—one in permanent combat and one in permanent support. Large numbers of non-combat positions must be available to which combat troops can return for duty before being redeployed.

The point was repeated in specific findings. In sum, Congress carefully evaluated the testimony that 80,000 women conscripts could be usefully employed in the event of a draft, and rejected it in the permissible exercise of its constitutional responsibility. The District Court was quite wrong in undertaking an independent evaluation of this evidence, rather than adopting an appropriately deferential examination of *Congress'* evaluation of that evidence.

In light of the foregoing, we conclude that Congress acted well within its constitutional authority when it authorized the registration of men, and not women, under the Military Selective Service Act. The decision of the District Court holding otherwise is accordingly

Reversed.

> "The Court's decision is inconsistent
> with the Constitution's guarantee of
> equal protection of the laws."

Dissenting Opinion:
The Military Selective Service
Act Is Unconstitutional

Thurgood Marshall

Thurgood Marshall was a Supreme Court justice from 1967 to 1991. He was the first African American to serve on the Court.

In the following excerpt from Marshall's dissent in the 1981 case of Rostker v. Goldberg, *the justice claims that the Court erred in deferring to Congress by upholding the male-only requirement of the Military Selective Service Act as constitutional. Marshall contends that all legislation needs to comply with the U.S. Constitution and that, in this case, it does not. He contends that Congress did not justify the necessity of restricting mandatory military registration to males. Furthermore, he argues, the Court's focus on the issue of women in combat ignores the fact that the legislation in question only deals with registration.*

The Court today places its imprimatur [approval] on one of the most potent remaining public expressions of "ancient canards about the proper role of women" [*Phillips v. Martin Marietta Corp.* (1971)]. It upholds a statute that requires males, but not females, to register for the draft, and which thereby categorically excludes women from a funda-

Thurgood Marshall, dissenting opinion, *Rostker v. Goldberg*, U.S. Supreme Court, June 25, 1981.

mental civic obligation. Because I believe the Court's decision is inconsistent with the Constitution's guarantee of equal protection of the laws, I dissent. . . .

Gender-Based Classifications

By now it should be clear that statutes like the MSSA [Military Selective Service Act], which discriminate on the basis of gender, must be examined under the "heightened" scrutiny mandated by *Craig v. Boren* (1976). Under this test, a gender-based classification cannot withstand constitutional challenge unless the classification is substantially related to the achievement of an important governmental objective. This test applies whether the classification discriminates against males or females. The party defending the challenged classification carries the burden of demonstrating both the importance of the governmental objective it serves and the substantial relationship between the discriminatory means and the asserted end. Consequently, before we can sustain the MSSA, the Government must demonstrate that the gender-based classification it employs bears "a close and substantial relationship to [the achievement of] important governmental objectives" [*Personnel Administrator of Massachusetts v. Feeney* (1979)].

The MSSA states that "an adequate armed strength must be achieved and maintained to insure the security of this Nation." I agree with the majority that "[n]o one could deny that . . . the Government's interest in raising and supporting armies is an 'important governmental interest.'" Consequently, the first part of the *Craig v. Boren* test is satisfied. But the question remains whether the discriminatory means employed itself substantially serves the statutory end. In concluding that it does, the Court correctly notes that Congress enacted (and reactivated) the MSSA pursuant to its constitutional authority to raise and maintain armies. The majority also notes that "the Court accords 'great weight to the decisions of Congress,'" and that the Court has accorded particular deference to decisions arising in the context of Congress authority over military affairs. I have no particular quarrel with these sentiments in the majority opinion. I simply add that even in the area of military affairs, deference to congressional judgments cannot be allowed to shade into an abdication of this Court's ultimate responsibility to decide constitutional questions. As the Court has pointed out:

> [T]he phrase "war power" cannot be invoked as a talismanic incantation to support any exercise of congressional power which can be brought within its ambit. "[E]ven the war power does not remove constitutional limitations safeguarding essential liberties." [*United States v. Robel* (1967).]

One such "safeguar[d] [of] essential liberties" is the Fifth Amendment's guarantee of equal protection of the laws. When, as here, a federal law that classifies on the basis of gender is challenged as violating this constitutional guarantee, it is ultimately for this Court, not Congress, to decide whether there exists the constitutionally required "close and substantial relationship" between the discriminatory means employed and the asserted governmental objective. In my judgment, there simply is no basis for concluding in this case that excluding women from registration is substantially related to the achievement of a concededly important governmental interest in maintaining an effective defense. The Court reaches a contrary conclusion only by using an "[a]nnounced degre[e] of 'deference' to legislative judgmen[t]" as a "facile abstractio[n] . . . to justify a result."

The Justification for Excluding Women

The Government does not defend the exclusion of women from registration on the ground that preventing women from serving in the military is substantially related to the effectiveness of the Armed Forces. Indeed, the successful experience of women serving in all branches of the Armed Services would belie any such claim. Some 150,000 women volunteers are presently on active service in the military, and their number is expected to increase to over 250,000 by 1985. At the congressional hearings, representatives of both the Department of Defense and the Armed Services testified that the participation of women in the All-Volunteer Armed Forces has contributed substantially to military effectiveness. Congress has never disagreed with the judgment of the military experts that women have made significant contributions to the effectiveness of the military. On the contrary, Congress has repeatedly praised the performance of female members of the Armed Forces, and has approved efforts by the Armed Services to expand their role. Just last year, the Senate Armed Services Committee declared:

> Women now volunteer for military service and are assigned to most military specialties. These volunteers now make an important contribution to our Armed Forces. The number of women in the military has increased significantly in the past few years, and is expected to continue to increase.

These statements thus make clear that Congress' decision to exclude women from registration—and therefore from a draft drawing on the pool of registrants—cannot rest on a supposed need to prevent women from serving in the Armed Forces. The justification for the MSSA's gender-based discrimination must therefore be found in considerations that are peculiar to the objectives of registration.

The most authoritative discussion of Congress' reasons for declining to require registration of women is contained in the Report prepared by the Senate Armed Services Committee on the Fiscal Year 1981 Defense Authorization Bill. The Report's findings were endorsed by the House-Senate Conferees on the Authorization Bill. Both Houses of Congress subsequently adopted the findings by passing the Conference Report. As the majority notes, the Report's "findings are in effect findings of the entire Congress." The Senate Report sets out the objectives Congress sought to accomplish by excluding women from registration, and this Court may appropriately look to the Report in evaluating the justification for the discrimination.

Women and Combat

According to the Senate Report "[t]he policy precluding the use of women in combat is . . . the most important reason for not including women in a registration system." In reaffirming the combat restrictions, the Report declared:

> Registering women for assignment to combat or assigning women to combat positions in peacetime then would leave the actual performance of sexually mixed units as an experiment to be conducted in war with unknown risk—a risk that the committee finds militarily unwarranted and dangerous. Moreover, the committee feels that any attempt to assign women to combat positions could affect the national resolve at the time of mobilization, a time of great strain on all aspects of the Nation's resources.

Had appellees raised a constitutional challenge to the prohibition against assignment of women to combat, this discussion in the Senate Report might well provide persuasive reasons for upholding the restrictions. But the validity of the combat restrictions is not an issue we need decide in this case. Moreover, since the combat restrictions on women have already been accomplished through statutes and policies that remain in force whether or not women are required to register or to be drafted, including women in registration and draft plans will not result in their being assigned to combat roles. Thus, even assuming that precluding the use of women in combat is an important governmental interest in its own right, there can be no suggestion that the exclusion of women from registration and a draft is substantially related to the achievement of this goal. . . .

The Registration of Women

Nothing in the Senate Report supports the Court's intimation that women must be excluded from registration because combat eligibility is a prerequisite for all the positions that would need to be filled in the event of a draft. The Senate Report concluded only that "[i]f mobilization were to be ordered in a wartime scenario, the *primary* manpower need would be for combat replacements" (emphasis added). This conclusion was in keeping with the testimony presented at the congressional hearings. The Department of Defense indicated that, in the event of a mobilization requiring reinstitution of the draft, the primary manpower requirement would be for combat troops and support personnel who can readily be deployed into combat. But the Department indicated that conscripts would also be needed to staff a variety of support positions having no prerequisite of combat eligibility, and which therefore could be filled by women. Assistant Secretary of Defense (Manpower, Reserve Affairs, and Logistics) [Robert B.] Pirie [Jr.] explained:

> Not only will we need to expand combat arms, and as I said, that is the most pressing need, but we also will need to expand the support establishment at the same time to allow the combat arms to carry out their function successfully. The support establishment now uses women very effectively, and, in wartime, I think the same would be true.

In testifying about the Defense Department's reasons for concluding that women should be included in registration plans, Pirie stated:

> It is in the interest of national security that, in an emergency requiring the conscription for military service of the Nation's youth, the best qualified people for a wide variety of tasks in our Armed Forces be available. The performance of women in our Armed Forces today strongly supports the conclusion that many of the best qualified people for some military jobs in the 18–26 age category will be women.

The Defense Department also concluded that there are no military reasons that would justify excluding women from registration. The Department's position was described to Congress in these terms:

Our conclusion is that there are good reasons for registering [women]. Our conclusion is *even more strongly that there are not good reasons for refusing to register them.*

All four Service Chiefs agreed that there are no military reasons for refusing to register women, and uniformly advocated requiring registration of women. The military's position on the issue was summarized by then Army Chief of Staff General Rogers:

[W]omen should be required to register for the reason that [Marine Corps commandant] General [Louis] Wilson mentioned, which is in order for us to have an inventory of what the available strength is within the military qualified pool in this country. . . .

The Military Need for Women

This review of the findings contained in the Senate Report and the testimony presented at the congressional hearings demonstrates that there is no basis for the Court's representation that women are ineligible for all the positions that would need to be filled in the event of a draft. Testimony about personnel requirements in the event of a draft established that women could fill at least 80,000 of the 650,000 positions for which conscripts would be inducted. Thus, with respect to these 80,000 or more positions, the statutes and policies barring women from combat do not provide a reason for distinguishing between male and female potential conscripts; the two groups are, in the majority's parlance, "similarly situated." As such, the combat restrictions cannot by themselves supply the constitutionally required justification for the MSSA's gender-based classification. Since the classification precludes women from being drafted to fill positions for which they would be qualified and useful, the Government must demonstrate that excluding women from those positions is substantially related to the achievement of an important governmental objective.

The Government argues, however, that the "consistent testimony before Congress was to the effect that there is *no military need* to draft women." And the Government points to a statement in the Senate Report that

> [b]oth the civilian and military leadership agreed that there was no military need to draft women ... The argument for registration and induction of women ... is not based on military necessity, but on considerations of equity.

In accepting the Government's contention, the Court asserts that the Presidents decision to seek authority to register women was based on "equity," and concludes that

> Congress was certainly entitled, in the exercise of its constitutional powers to raise and regulate armies and navies, to focus on the question of military need, rather than "equity."

In my view, a more careful examination of the concepts of "equity" and "military need" is required. . . .

To be sure, there is no "military need" to draft women in the sense that a war could be waged without their participation. This fact is, however, irrelevant to resolving the constitutional issue. As previously noted, it is not appellees' burden to prove that registration of women substantially furthers the objectives of the MSSA. Rather, because eligibility for combat is not a requirement for some of the positions to be filled in the event of a draft, it is incumbent on the Government to show that excluding women from a draft to fill those positions substantially furthers an important governmental objective.

It may be, however, that the Senate Report's allusion to "military need" is meant to convey Congress' expectation that women volunteers will make it unnecessary to draft any women. The majority apparently accepts this meaning when it states:

Congress also concluded that, whatever the need for women for noncombat roles during mobilization, whether 80,000 or less, it could be met by volunteers.

But since the purpose of registration is to protect against unanticipated shortages of volunteers, it is difficult to see how excluding women from registration can be justified by conjectures about the expected number of female volunteers. I fail to see why the exclusion of a pool of persons who would be conscripted only *if needed* can be justified by reference to the current supply of volunteers. In any event, the Defense Department's best estimate is that, in the event of a mobilization requiring reinstitution of the draft, there will not be enough women volunteers to fill the positions for which women would be eligible. The Department told Congress:

If we had a mobilization, our present best projection is that we could use women in some 80,000 of the jobs we would be *inducting* 650,000 people for.

Thus, however the "military need" statement in the Senate Report is understood, it does not provide the constitutionally required justification for the total exclusion of women from registration and draft plans.

Recognizing the need to go beyond the "military need" argument, the Court asserts that

Congress determined that staffing noncombat positions with women during a mobilization would be positively detrimental to the important goal of military flexibility.

None would deny that preserving "military flexibility" is an important governmental interest. But to justify the exclusion of women from registration and the draft on this ground, there must be a further showing that staffing even a limited number of noncombat positions with women would impede military flexibility. I find nothing in the Senate Report to provide any basis for the Court's representation that Congress believed this to be the case. . . .

The Court's Review of Congress

After reviewing the discussion and findings contained in the Senate Report, the most I am able to say of the Report is that it demonstrates that drafting *very large numbers* of women would frustrate the achievement of a number of important governmental objectives that relate to the ultimate goal of maintaining "an adequate armed strength . . . to insure the security of this Nation." Or to put it another way, the Senate Report establishes that induction of a large number of men, but only a limited number of women, as determined by the military's personnel requirements, would be substantially related to important governmental interests. But the discussion and findings in the Senate Report do not enable the Government to carry its burden of demonstrating that *completely* excluding women from the draft by excluding them from registration substantially furthers important governmental objectives.

In concluding that the Government has carried its burden in this case, the Court adopts "an appropriately deferential examination of *Congress'* evaluation of the evidence." The majority then proceeds to supplement Congress' actual findings with those the Court apparently believes Congress could (and should) have made. Beyond that, the Court substitutes hollow shibboleths [catchphrase] about "deference to legislative decisions" for constitutional analysis. It is as if the majority has lost sight of the fact that "it is the responsibility of this Court to act as the ultimate interpreter of the Constitution" [*Powell v. McCormack* (1969)]. Congressional enactments in the area of military affairs must, like all other laws, be *judged* by the standards of the Constitution. For the Constitution is the supreme law of the land, and *all* legislation must conform to the principles it lays down. As the Court has pointed out,

> the phrase "war power" cannot be invoked as a talismanic incantation to support any exercise of congressional power which can be brought within its ambit. [*United States v. Robel* (1967).]

Furthermore,

> [w]hen it appears that an Act of Congress conflicts with [a constitutional] provisio[n], we have no choice but to enforce the paramount commands of the Constitution. We are sworn to do no less. We cannot push back the limits of the Constitution merely to accommodate challenged legislation. [*Trop v. Dulles* (1958).]

In some 106 instances since this Court was established, it has determined that congressional action exceeded the bounds of the Constitution. I believe the same is true of this statute. In an attempt to avoid its constitutional obligation, the Court today "pushes back the limits of the Constitution" to accommodate an Act of Congress.

"*Congress should change the law to reflect that in a time of need, America may draw upon the talents and abilities of all of its citizens who are otherwise eligible for military service.*"

Congress Should End the Male-Only Registration Upheld in *Rostker*

Scott E. Dunn

Major Scott E. Dunn is associate professor of administrative law at the Judge Advocate General's Legal Center and School of the U.S. Army in Charlottesville, Virginia.

In the following excerpt, Dunn argues that the portion of the Military Selective Service Act (MSSA) that only requires registration by males—a requirement upheld as constitutional by the Supreme Court in Rostker v. Goldberg—*needs to be changed by Congress to also require registration by females. Dunn contends that the justification for only requiring men to register, based on the fact that women are excluded from combat, fails since most military positions are in support rather than in combat. Dunn believes that the Court's decision in* Rostker *requires that the MSSA be changed by legislation rather than judicial action, as has been illustrated by a recent unsuccessful court challenge to the gender-based classification of the MSSA.*

The Military Selective Service Act (MSSA) requires male citizens and legal residents between the ages of eighteen and twenty-six to register for possible conscription in the

Scott E. Dunn, "The Military Selective Service Act's Exemption of Women: It is Time to End It," *Army Lawyer*, April 2009.

event of a draft. Women are exempt from this requirement. The MSSA exempts women primarily because the draft has been viewed as a mechanism for rapidly inducting troops into combat positions from which women have traditionally been excluded.

Although the exclusion of women from ground combat roles continues, a large majority of military occupational specialties (MOSs) and duty positions are open to women in today's all-volunteer force. Possible shortages of military recruits are not likely to be limited to combat MOSs and duty positions from which women are excluded. On the contrary, a majority of male conscripts, though eligible for duty in ground combat, would presumably fill positions that could also be filled by women. This is so simply because most military positions are in the support branches, rather than in combat arms.

The time has come for Congress to reconsider its narrow view of the draft as a means only of augmenting combat troop strength. Congress should broaden the intended purpose of the MSSA to include augmenting troop strength in combat support and combat service support roles in which women are eligible to serve. There is little reason to eschew half of the pool of potential recruits, nor to exempt that half of the population from its civic obligations. This proposed change does not rely on any change in current policy regarding the assignment of women to combat positions, but any broadening of the assignment opportunities available to women would only underline the desirability and equity of subjecting women to MSSA registration requirements. . . .

The Court's Decision in *Rostker*

The most significant legal challenge to the MSSA's exemption of women made its way to the U.S. Supreme Court after the registration requirement was reinstated in 1980. In *Rostker v. Goldberg* [1981], the Court upheld the exemption of women from the MSSA. The plaintiffs in *Rostker* were men subject to registration and conscription during in the early 1970s, who alleged that the MSSA's application solely to men violated their due process rights under the Constitution.

The case lay dormant for several years after the draft and registration requirements were suspended, but it had not been dismissed. Litigation recommenced in 1979 when the defendants attempted to dismiss the claim in district court and were unsuccessful. The U.S. District Court for the Eastern District of Pennsylvania did not initially rule on the merits of the claim because it lacked sufficient facts on the record. After the facts were better developed, the district court ultimately ruled in favor of the plaintiffs regarding their constitutional claim and enjoined the Government from commencing registration. The Director of Selective Service immediately appealed and the injunction was stayed pending resolution of the case by the Supreme Court.

The Supreme Court held that men and women were not similarly situated with respect to a draft that purports to focus on filling combat positions from which women are excluded. Because of this exclusion, the exemption of women from the reach of the MSSA was closely related to Congress' purpose in authorizing draft registration and did not violate the Due Process Clause of the Constitution. The alleged victims of discrimination in this case were men, not women, because while the MSSA placed obligations upon men and exempted women, it did not exclude women from voluntary military service.

The Court's majority opinion did not clearly state the controlling legal standard that should be applied to the MSSA's exemption of women. The Court emphasized its deference to Congress in the realm of military policy. It certainly deferred to Congress' characterization of the purpose of the draft, which was to supply combat troops. However, the Court stopped short of agreeing with the Solicitor General's argument that the gender distinction in question should be judged under the lowest form of constitutional scrutiny normally reserved for military matters, which is whether the statute in question is rationally related to a legitimate governmental purpose. Likewise, the Court did not necessarily refuse to apply the heightened form of scrutiny articulated in *Craig v. Boren* [1976] for gender-based distinctions, which requires that gender-based discrimination be "substantially related to important governmental interest." Instead, the Court stated:

> We do not think that the substantive guarantees of due process or certainty in the law will be advanced by any further "refinement" in the applicable tests as suggested by the Government. Announced degrees of "deference" to legislative judgments, just as levels of "scrutiny" which this Court announces that it applies to particular classifications made by a legislative body, may all too readily become facile abstractions used to justify a result. In this case the courts are called upon to decide whether Congress, acting under an explicit constitutional grant of authority, has by that action transgressed an explicit guarantee of individual rights which limits the authority so conferred. Simply labeling the legislative decision "military" on the one hand or "gender-based" on the other does not automatically guide a court to the correct constitutional result.

While the Court did not choose between these competing standards, it stated that MSSA's exemption of women nevertheless satisfied them both. The opinion implicitly rejected any higher, "strict scrutiny" standard for the gender-based distinction. Essentially, the opinion states that no clear standard applies, but that the MSSA would survive scrutiny under any test that could reasonably be applied.

Dissenting Opinions in *Rostker*

Justices [Byron] White and [Thurgood] Marshall wrote dissenting opinions, each noting that draftees would not be exclusively used to fill combat positions. Both noted that while the primary purpose of a draft may be to provide combat troops who had to be male, some of the men drafted would be used in non-combat roles. Justice White pointed out an apparent absurdity in the majority opinion, which at one point seemed to argue that the military required the flexibility to move non-combat troops into combat roles as necessary, thus providing another basis for drafting men exclusively. While this flexibility may indeed be helpful, Justice White noted that "if during mobilization for war, all non-combat military positions must be filled by combat-qualified personnel available to be moved into combat positions, there would be no occasion whatsoever to have any women in the Army, whether as volunteers or inductees." Justice White argued that the government had not shown that female draftees could not be usefully employed in non-combat roles, rather that it had merely relied on the administrative convenience of limiting the draft to individuals who could fill either combat or non-combat positions. In his view, this was not sufficient to justify the exemption of women.

Justice Marshall focused on the legislative history that revealed that the military services appeared to disagree with Congress, and in fact desired the registration of women. According to his review of the record, "[t]estimony about personnel requirements in the event of a draft established that women could fill at least 80,000 of the 650,000 positions for which conscripts would be inducted." He agreed that there would be no reason to register women if "it could be guaranteed in advance" that any future draft would only be used to fill positions from which women were excluded. That not being the case, however, he believed that the government had failed to demonstrate that the exemption of women was substantially related to the achievement of an important government interest.

The Court's opinion in *Rostker* appeared to settle the constitutional question involved. Moreover, the unlikely prospects for institution of the draft throughout the 1980s and 1990s probably muted opposition to Selective Service policies. Consequently, there appears to have been little active legal opposition to the exemption of women in the two decades following *Rostker*. That changed following the events of 11 September 2001.

A 2003 Challenge to *Rostker*

The most recent legal challenge of any significance occurred when the MSSA's exemption of women was challenged in *Schwartz v. Brodsky* in 2003. The plaintiffs brought suit in U.S. District Court for the District of Massachusetts. They challenged both the constitutionality of the MSSA and provisions of Massachusetts state law that penalized individuals who failed to comply with the MSSA regarding eligibility for state student financial aid.

The plaintiffs contended that military assignment policies for women had evolved to such a degree since *Rostker v. Goldberg* was decided in 1981 that the factual underpinning of *Rostker* had eroded. They argued that the expansion of military positions available to women had fundamentally changed the circumstances under which a future draft would be conducted. The district court granted summary judgment to the defendants, however, because the plaintiffs conceded that two essential facts had not changed: first, that the legislative purpose of the MSSA was still to provide for a draft of primarily combat troops; and second, that women were still excluded from combat positions. The court asserted that at least one of these essential facts would have to change in order to call *Rostker*'s holding into question. In granting the defendant's motion for summary judgment, the court wrote:

> [T]he Constitution expressly grants the power "to raise and support Armies," "to provide and maintain a Navy," and "to make Rules for the Government and Regulation of the land and naval Forces," . . . to Congress and not to the Judiciary. The Judiciary has neither the power nor the competence to

undertake these awesome responsibilities. . . . If a deeply rooted military tradition of male-only draft registration is to be ended, it should be accomplished by that branch of government which has the constitutional power to do so and which best represents the "consent of the governed"—the Congress of the United States, the elected representatives of the people.

Future Legal Challenges

Legal challenges similar to *Schwartz v. Brodsky* can be expected to continue. For example, Harvey Schwartz, the plaintiff's attorney in *Schwartz* is currently representing an Internal Revenue Service employee who was fired due to his failure to comply with registration requirements under the MSSA. Regarding *Rostker*, Mr. Schwartz stated, "that decision was based on the status of women in the military at the time, and it's a whole new world now."

It is doubtful that the changes in this "new world" will warrant a reversal of *Rostker*, though they may invite further litigation. As the *Schwartz* court noted, *Rostker* is likely to remain valid case law so long as women are prohibited from combat positions, however those positions are defined by DoD [U.S. Department of Defense] policy, and as long as Congress views the draft as primarily a means of providing combat troops. Any change in the MSSA registration requirements, therefore, is more likely to come from legislative action than a judicial decision. . . .

Congress should change the law to reflect that in a time of need, America may draw upon the talents and abilities of all of its citizens who are otherwise eligible for military service. The American ethic is essentially egalitarian, and so too should be our system of conscription. The evolution of our conscription laws towards greater inclusion and the fairest possible allocation of duties and responsibilities demands the inclusion of women. This change, however, does not appear to be required by the Constitution and therefore cannot and should not be mandated by the judiciary. As the court wisely noted in *Schwartz v. Brodsky*, the tradition of male-only conscription is best changed if that reflects the will of the people as expressed through Congress.

"Judicial deference recognizes that federal civilian courts are not empowered or capable of making policy for the armed forces."

The Judicial Deference Shown to the Military in *Rostker* Should Continue

Elaine Donnelly

Elaine Donnelly is founder and president of the Center for Military Readiness, an independent public policy organization that specializes in military personnel issues.

In the following article, Donnelly says that steps need to be taken to ensure that the courts do not dictate military policy. She argues that the Supreme Court was correct in its Rostker v. Goldberg *decision, wherein it deferred to the legislature and upheld the male-only registration requirement of the Military Selective Service Act. Donnelly believes that the Court needs to have judges who will continue this tradition of judicial deference to legislation regarding the military, and she urges Congress to make sure that legislation is written in a manner that prevents judicial review on military policy in the future.*

During upcoming hearings on the nomination of Judge John Roberts to the Supreme Court, senators should inquire about the nominee's philosophy on the tradition of ju-

Elaine Donnelly, "Courts, Congress, and the Military," *Washington Times*, August 8, 2005. Reproduced by permission.

dicial deference to the military. They should also make sure Judge Roberts does not agree with retiring Justice Sandra Day O'Connor that foreign court rulings may be used as guidance in U.S. courts.

These constitutional principles will greatly affect issues of concern to civilians as well as the military. Examples include the constitutionality of women's exemption from Selective Service registration, religious practices at military installations and service academies, the law banning homosexuals from the military, and the Solomon Amendment—legislation that withholds government funds from colleges that discriminate against military recruiters.

Inquiries about these matters will illuminate the nominee's judicial philosophy, while reminding Congress of the importance of passing clearly written laws for the military, and overseeing faithful enforcement reflecting legislative intent.

A History of Deference

The concept of deference to the military is rooted in Article I of the Constitution, which vests in Congress the power to raise and support forces for national defense. Judicial deference recognizes that federal civilian courts are not empowered or capable of making policy for the armed forces, which are governed by unique rules and policies that necessitate a different application of constitutional rights.

The landmark 1981 decision in *Rostker v. Goldberg*, for example, found Selective Service registration of 18-year-old men, but not women, does not violate equal protection standards. In *Rostker*, the Supreme Court recognized a military draft is only instituted to provide a pool of "combat replacements" in time of war, and it would be problematic to register women for land combat from which they are exempt.

In 2003, five Boston students, represented by counsel associated with the American Civil Liberties Union [ACLU], challenged the *Rostker* precedent in a Massachusetts federal court.

The opinion dismissing that lawsuit restated the historic nexus between Selective Service obligations and land combat assignments, and deferred to the military's judgment.

The court also reaffirmed the judiciary has neither the power nor the competence to make policy in this area. A future Supreme Court adhering to this principle is unlikely to reverse the *Rostker* precedent, but this could change due to unauthorized policy shifts on involving women in land combat.

A Confused Policy

Under current Defense Department rules, female soldiers are not assigned to land combat forces such as the infantry, or support units that constantly operate, or "collocate," with combat troops that deliberately engage the enemy. If the Pentagon wants to change these regulations, federal law mandates advance notice to Congress, accompanied by an analysis of the effect of proposed revisions on women's exemption from Selective Service obligations.

Army officials have used semantic sophistry to circumvent the notification law, while deploying female soldiers in smaller land combat-collocated support units still required to be all-male. House Armed Services Committee Chairman Duncan Hunter, California Republican, saw through the quibbling, and led the full committee in approving legislation to codify current policy on women in land combat. Instead of getting the Army back in line, Defense Secretary Donald Rumsfeld intervened to stifle Mr. Hunter's efforts.

Offensive land combat missions are unchanged. But Army officials have increased confusion by blurring "combat" to include almost any soldier in a danger zone. Future judges ready to defer to the military's judgment on women in combat will have difficulty determining what the policy is. Ambiguity invites another ACLU challenge to women's exemption from registering for the draft, which now is on shaky ground.

The same confusion threatens the 1993 law that excludes homosexuals from the military. Contrary to most news accounts, Congress rejected former President [Bill] Clinton's proposal to accommodate discreet homosexuals in uniform, known as "don't ask, don't tell." The Clinton Defense Department nevertheless incorporated the concept in regulations to enforce the law.

In 1996, the U.S. 4th Circuit Court of Appeals upheld the law's constitutionality, but recognized Mr. Clinton's "don't ask, don't tell" policy/regulations were inconsistent with it. Homosexual activists will exploit the contradiction to achieve their goals. To which military policy—exclusion or accommodation—will a future Supreme Court defer?

The Opinions of Foreign Courts

Complicating matters further, some justices have started citing foreign court opinions in cases such as *Lawrence v. Texas*. In that 2004 ruling, Justice Anthony Kennedy cited foreign court opinions in a controversial decision that overturned previous legal precedent and all state laws banning sodomy.

The *Lawrence* decision quoted an amicus brief filed by Human Rights Watch, which referred to a 1981 ruling of the European Court of Human Rights in Strasbourg, France, which upheld homosexual rights (*Dudgeon v. the United Kingdom*). The amicus brief shrewdly did not mention another decision by the same European Court in 1999, which ordered Britain to accept homosexuals in the military (*Lustig-Prean and Beckett v. the United Kingdom*).

The Web sites of Human Rights Watch and the ACLU have posted articles outlining determined plans to use the second European Court ruling, combined with the *Lawrence v. Texas* precedent, as battering rams to bring down America's ban on homosexuals in the military. The resulting social turmoil could greatly undermine morale in the volunteer force.

The armed forces should remain under civilian control, but not that of activist judges quoting foreign courts. Congressional power to make policy for the military creates a corollary responsibility to write clear legislation and oversee faithful enforcement. Unresolved confusion invites overreaching Supreme Court decisions that have damaged many American institutions. The [George W.] Bush administration and Congress must ensure that our military does not become one of them.

"Deference is very much inconsistent with the military's own institutional values, and . . . [it] has done a great deal of harm to the military's sense of professional ethics."

The Judicial Deference Shown to the Military in *Rostker* Should End

Diane H. Mazur

Diane H. Mazur is professor of law and the Gerald A. Sohn Research Scholar at the University of Florida, Levin College of Law. She specializes in civil-military relations under the Constitution.

In the following selection, Mazur argues that judicial deference to military policy needs to end. She claims that the Supreme Court's decision in Rostker v. Goldberg, *upholding the male-only registration requirement of the Military Selective Service Act, is based on obsolete facts and law. According to Mazur, the judicial deference to the military supported by* Rostker *stems from cultural facts and not facts of the U.S. Constitution. She concludes that the view of the military that supports the policy of judicial deference needs to change.*

It is clear that judicial deference in matters related to the military has been a tremendous burden in challenging "Don't Ask, Don't Tell." What is unusual is that this doctrine

Diane H. Mazur, "Harvard Law School Lambda Second Annual Gay and Lesbian Legal Advocacy Conference: 'Don't Ask, Don't Tell,' Panel Three: The Contours of Judicial Deference to Military Personnel Policies," *Duke Journal of Gender Law & Policy*, vol. 14, May 2007, pp. 1238–40. Copyright © 2007 Duke University School of Law. Reproduced by permission.

is treated as longstanding and beyond question, even though the case most often cited for the doctrine, *Rostker v. Goldberg*, was decided in 1981, and even though *Rostker* today is obsolete both on its facts and on its law. Yet there is something about *Rostker* that persists in a way that is out of proportion to any validity it still has.

The Relevance of *Rostker*

The facts of *Rostker* are completely obsolete today. Congress has repealed the federal statutes that barred women from combat service at sea and in the air. The Defense Department's definition of combat service on the ground has changed so completely that today, even in the Army and the Marine Corps, a majority of positions can be filled by women. It would be very difficult for a court today to rule, as *Rostker* did, that women would be of little use to the military in time of war.

Much of the law of *Rostker* is also obsolete today. In *United States v. Virginia* [1996], the Court held that classifications on the basis of sex must be supported by an exceedingly persuasive justification. It would be very difficult for a court today to slide by, as did *Rostker*, an enhanced standard of scrutiny in an equal-protection case.

The only thing that survives from *Rostker* is its statement about the doctrine of judicial deference in matters concerning the military. This aspect of *Rostker*—this one lingering aspect of *Rostker*—has been absolutely tenacious in its effect on the law in this area. Twenty-six years later we're still arguing the platitudes of *Rostker*, even though those platitudes have been completely divorced from facts and divorced from law. Yet the platitudes live on. . . .

"Congress is not free to disregard the Constitution." And then the opposing side will argue, "Judges are not given the task of running the Army."

A Cultural Phenomenon

I believe that this is the problem: Courts follow the *culture* of *Rostker* much more than the *law* of *Rostker*. Judicial deference to the military is primarily a cultural phenomenon, not a legal one, and that is why it is so difficult to displace. That is why it's so difficult to argue against, because you're no longer arguing law, you're arguing culture.

The traditional form of judicial deference in cases involving the military, going back to the Civil War, only applied to jurisdictional questions of whether a civilian federal court could review or overturn the judgment of a court-martial. That's it.

It is only in the post-Vietnam era that judicial deference has been used to uphold policies that affect . . . entire groups of people rather than individual determinations that are made on specific facts and specific situations with specific people.

Rostker resonates so strongly today because it is an accurate statement about the way we view the military today. It's not an accurate statement about judicial deference or about constitutional structure or about anything else. It is a statement of the way we as Americans understand our relationship to our military. And these themes have completely replaced any consideration of the history of deference, the purpose of deference, and the consequences of deference.

We usually discuss deference in terms of the effect that it has on gay service members or on women or on other people who are challenging military policy, but today I would like to talk about the effect that deference has on the military. And my argument today will be that deference is very much inconsistent with the military's own institutional values, and over the last generation, judicial deference has done a great deal of harm to the military's sense of professional ethics.

Justifications for Judicial Deference

Judicial deference as a general matter, not just confined to the military but as a general matter, is usually justified on the basis of several factors: greater expertise, greater accountability, and some sort of enhanced benefit to the institution to which we defer.

Unlike other situations in which courts defer, though, the doctrine of judicial deference involving the military sometimes fails to respect the military's own expertise. Judicial deference is this infinitely flexible doctrine. It can apply to decisions made by the military. It can apply to decisions made by the Department of Defense. It can apply to decisions made by Congress.

Interestingly, though, it is not necessarily related to military expertise. Most people assume that in *Rostker* the military was resisting drafting women, because that's the way the case came out. In *Rostker*, however, the military very much wanted to draft women, because they said that is the way we will know where the qualified people are if we need them.

Congress disagreed, and the doctrine of judicial deference, oddly enough, was used to overrule what the military thought was the best thing to do as a matter of military expertise.

Professional military expertise is a factor in judicial deference only when the military happens to agree, as it did with "Don't Ask, Don't Tell."

Second, the doctrine of deference works best when there's an appropriate level of accountability for the decisions that are made. And of course defenders of deference point to the democratic accountability of Congress and the President when they deny courts a role in these cases.

In the context of constitutional equality, though, reliance on democratic accountability is going to be inherently ineffective, and our reliance today on an all-volunteer military only makes the problem worse.

The Court, when it makes rulings in cases like *Rostker* and on "Don't Ask, Don't Tell," is able to confine the impact of deference to the very small segment of America who serves in the military. As a matter of accountability, deference would make a whole lot more sense if we had a draft military, because unconstitutional policies would affect citizens much more broadly than they do today.

Third, and I think the most important point, is deference should apply in a way that doesn't harm the institution to which we're supposedly deferring. And my argument today is that deference has done great damage to the military over the last generation. It has taught service members and also civilians—it has taught all of us—some very bad lessons over the last generation.

Bad Lessons

The first bad lesson is that the military is a separate society.... It is distant from and it is inaccessible to civilians, and therefore civilians cannot understand it (at least when those civilians are judges, I suppose).

The second bad lesson: The law does not apply to the military the same way it applies to everyone else.

Third bad lesson: Military values are morally superior to constitutional values. Constitutional values are inconsistent with military effectiveness.

Fourth bad lesson: Civilians should be reluctant to question military policy, and service members should be resentful when they do. Military service involves a sense of duty and discipline that is beyond the capability of the average American, and so military policy need not be justified to the average American in the same way that other government policies are.

And last, and perhaps the worst lesson of them all, is that political partisanship sometimes works better for the military than its traditional professional ethic of political neutrality, because the military now understands that its expertise receives the most respect when it happens to be politically useful to the majority. I don't need to remind you of some recent instances in which that bad lesson has been illustrated.

All of these lessons, all of these bad lessons, are inconsistent with ethical traditions of military service.

The View of the Military

In conclusion, it will be difficult to dislodge the doctrine of judicial deference until we change the culture of our civil-military relations—until we change the culture of how view the military in this country.

Deference is a convenient mechanism for expressing our cultural reluctance to engage military issues and our reluctance to actively participate in civilian control of the military. And this is why I think it is so important for law schools and other institutions of law to actively engage the military and actively engage issues of military law, and not only issues related to "Don't Ask, Don't Tell." That kind of active engagement is the only way that we're going to dislodge a doctrine like judicial deference in matters involving the military.

CHAPTER 2

Employment Decisions Influenced by Gender Stereotypes Are Discriminatory

Case Overview

Price Waterhouse v. Hopkins (1989)

In *Price Waterhouse v. Hopkins*, the U.S. Supreme Court determined that an employer's consideration of sex or gender in employment decisions violates Title VII of the Civil Rights Act of 1964, even when gender is not the sole reason for its employment decision. Title VII prohibits discrimination by employers on the basis of race, color, religion, sex, or national origin. When Ann Hopkins was denied partnership by the professional services firm Price Waterhouse in 1982, she accused the company of sex discrimination under Title VII.

In consideration of Hopkins's candidacy, Price Waterhouse partners had praised her accomplishments and professional skills but had criticized her interpersonal skills in such a manner that pointed to her gender. One partner had described her as "macho," another said that she "overcompensated for being a woman," another suggested she take "a course at charm school," and another advised her to "walk more femininely, talk more femininely, dress more femininely, wear make-up, have her hair styled, and wear jewelry." Lower courts concluded that the gender-based evaluations of Hopkins constituted discrimination based on sex, in violation of Title VII.

Prior to the *Price Waterhouse* decision, parties who had brought cases to the U.S. Supreme Court under Title VII had argued that the prohibited characteristic involved in employment decisions was either the sole reason for the employment decision or that it played no role at all. What set *Price Waterhouse* apart was that both parties agreed that gender was part of the decision—what is known as a mixed-motives case—and so the question for the Court was whether Price Waterhouse violated Title VII if it could show that it would have made the same decision without taking gender into account. The divided Court, in a plurality opinion by William J. Brennan Jr., concluded that it was a violation of Title VII to take gender into account in employment decisions, but also held that the employer could avoid liability if it could prove by a preponderance of evidence that it would have made the same adverse employment decision without taking gender into account. What was key about this case is that the Court's decision shifted the burden of proof in such mixed-motive cases to the employer to show that its action was not discriminatory, rather than requiring the employee to prove discrimination. The Supreme Court agreed with the ultimate findings of the lower courts but disagreed with the reasoning used to arrive at this finding.

There was wide disagreement on the Court about the decision in *Price Waterhouse*, leading to one plurality opinion and two concurring opinions, with no majority opinion in the case. Anthony Kennedy's dissent criticized the Court for shifting the burden of proof to employers in cases such as Hopkins's. Congress disagreed with the Court's view that an employer could avoid all liability by proving it would make the same decision without taking gender or sex into account: The Civil Rights Act of 1991 prohibits the consideration of race, color, religion, sex, or national origin in employment decisions, even if the decision would have been the same without consideration of those factors. Nonetheless, the legacy of *Price Waterhouse* continues to be relevant today insofar as it recognized that sex-role stereotyping constitutes sex discrimination. Such reasoning has been used in several cases since *Price Waterhouse* in finding that discrimination of transsexuals constitutes sex discrimination, including the case of *Smith v. Salem, Ohio, et al.* (6th Cir. 2004), discussed in Chapter 4.

> "When a plaintiff . . . proves that her gender played a motivating part in an employment decision, the defendant . . . [must prove] that it would have made the same decision even if it had not taken the plaintiff's gender into account."

Plurality Opinion: Employers Must Prove That Sex Stereotyping Did Not Influence an Employment Decision

William J. Brennan Jr.

William J. Brennan Jr. was a justice of the U.S. Supreme Court from 1956 to 1990. He was an outspoken liberal and is considered to be one of the more influential justices to have sat on the Court.

The following selection is from the 1989 Supreme Court case Price Waterhouse v. Hopkins, *wherein the Supreme Court ruled that it is a violation of Title VII of the Civil Rights Act of 1964 for gender to play a role in employment decisions. Title VII prohibits discrimination by employers on the basis of sex, among other things. In* Price Waterhouse v. Hopkins, *the Court determined that if a plaintiff shows that gender played a part in an employment decision, the employer may avoid liability only if it can show a preponderance of the evidence that it would have*

William J. Brennan Jr., plurality opinion, *Price Waterhouse v. Hopkins*, U.S. Supreme Court, May 1, 1989.

made the same decision regardless of gender. The Court thereby rejected the lower courts' approach that allowed Price Waterhouse to avoid liability by showing "clear and convincing evidence," making the requirement for evidence disputing the claim of sex discrimination more stringent.

At Price Waterhouse, a nationwide professional accounting partnership, a senior manager becomes a candidate for partnership when the partners in her local office submit her name as a candidate. All of the other partners in the firm are then invited to submit written comments on each candidate—either on a "long" or a "short" form, depending on the partner's degree of exposure to the candidate. Not every partner in the firm submits comments on every candidate. After reviewing the comments and interviewing the partners who submitted them, the firm's Admissions Committee makes a recommendation to the Policy Board. This recommendation will be either that the firm accept the candidate for partnership, put her application on "hold," or deny her the promotion outright. The Policy Board then decides whether to submit the candidate's name to the entire partnership for a vote, to "hold" her candidacy, or to reject her. The recommendation of the Admissions Committee, and the decision of the Policy Board, are not controlled by fixed guidelines: a certain number of positive comments from partners will not guarantee a candidate's admission to the partnership, nor will a specific quantity of negative comments necessarily defeat her application. Price Waterhouse places no limit on the number of persons, whom it will admit to the partnership in any given year.

Hopkins's Candidacy for Partnership

Ann Hopkins had worked at Price Waterhouse's Office of Government Services in Washington, D.C., for five years when the partners in that office proposed her as a candidate for partnership. Of the 662 partners at the firm at that time, 7 were women. Of the 88 persons proposed for partnership that year, only 1—Hopkins—was a woman. Forty-seven of these candidates were admitted to the partnership, 21 were rejected, and 20—including Hopkins—were "held" for reconsideration the following year. Thirteen of the 32 partners who had submitted comments on Hopkins supported her bid for partnership. Three partners recommended that her candidacy be placed on hold, eight stated that they did not have an informed opinion about her, and eight recommended that she be denied partnership.

In a jointly prepared statement supporting her candidacy, the partners in Hopkins' office showcased her successful 2-year effort to secure a $25 million contract with the Department of State, labeling it "an outstanding performance" and one that Hopkins carried out "virtually at the partner level." Despite Price Waterhouse's attempt at trial to minimize her contribution to this project, [District Court] Judge [Gerhard] Gesell specifically found that Hopkins had "played a key role in Price Waterhouse's successful effort to win a multimillion-dollar contract with the Department of State." Indeed, he went on,

> [n]one of the other partnership candidates at Price Waterhouse that year had a comparable record in terms of successfully securing major contracts for the partnership.

The partners in Hopkins' office praised her character as well as her accomplishments, describing her in their joint statement as "an outstanding professional" who had a "deft touch," a "strong character, independence and integrity." Clients appear to have agreed with these assessments. At trial, one official from the State Department described her as "extremely competent, intelligent," "strong and forthright, very productive, energetic and creative." Another high-ranking official praised Hopkins' decisiveness, broadmindedness, and "intellectual clarity"; she was, in his words, "a stimulating conversationalist." Evaluations such as these led Judge Gesell to conclude that Hopkins "had no difficulty dealing with clients and her clients appear to have been very pleased with her work" and that she was generally viewed as a highly competent project leader who worked long hours, pushed vigorously to meet deadlines and demanded much from the multidisciplinary staffs with which she worked.

On too many occasions, however, Hopkins' aggressiveness apparently spilled over into abrasiveness. Staff members seem to have borne the brunt of Hopkins' brusqueness. Long before her bid for partnership, partners evaluating her work had counseled her to improve her relations with staff members. Although later evaluations indicate an improvement, Hopkins' perceived shortcomings in this important area eventually doomed her bid for partnership. Virtually all of the partners' negative remarks about Hopkins—even those of partners supporting her—had to do with her "interpersonal skills." Both "[s]upporters and opponents of her candidacy," stressed Judge Gesell, "indicated that she was sometimes overly aggressive, unduly harsh, difficult to work with, and impatient with staff."

Evidence of Sex Stereotyping

There were clear signs, though, that some of the partners reacted negatively to Hopkins' personality because she was a woman. One partner described her as "macho"; another suggested that she "overcompensated for being a woman"; a third advised her to take "a course at charm school". Several partners criticized her use of profanity; in response, one partner suggested that those partners objected to her swearing only "because it's a lady using foul language." Another supporter explained that Hopkins

> ha[d] matured from a tough-talking somewhat masculine hard-nosed mgr [manager] to an authoritative, formidable, but much more appealing lady ptr [partner] candidate.

But it was the man who, as Judge Gesell found, bore responsibility for explaining to Hopkins the reasons for the Policy Board's decision to place her candidacy on hold who delivered the *coup de grace* [death blow]: in order to improve her chances for partnership, Thomas Beyer advised, Hopkins should "walk more femininely, talk more femininely, dress more femininely, wear make-up, have her hair styled, and wear jewelry." . . .

In previous years, other female candidates for partnership also had been evaluated in sex-based terms. As a general matter, Judge Gesell concluded, "[c]andidates were viewed favorably if partners believed they maintained their femin[in]ity while becoming effective professional managers"; in this environment, "[t]o be identified as a 'women's lib[b]er' was regarded as [a] negative comment." In fact, the judge found that, in previous years,

> [o]ne partner repeatedly commented that he could not consider any woman seriously as a partnership candidate, and believed that women were not even capable of functioning as senior managers—yet the firm took no action to discourage his comments, and recorded his vote in the overall summary of the evaluations.

Judge Gesell found that Price Waterhouse legitimately emphasized interpersonal skills in its partnership decisions, and also found that the firm had not fabricated its complaints about Hopkins' interpersonal skills as a pretext for discrimination. Moreover, he concluded, the firm did not give decisive emphasis to such traits only because Hopkins was a woman; although there were male candidates who lacked these skills but who were admitted to partnership, the judge found that these candidates possessed other, positive traits that Hopkins lacked.

The judge went on to decide, however, that some of the partners' remarks about Hopkins stemmed from an impermissibly cabined view of the proper behavior of women, and that Price Waterhouse had done nothing to disavow reliance on such comments. He held that Price Waterhouse had unlawfully discriminated against Hopkins on the basis of sex by consciously giving credence and effect to partners' comments that resulted from sex stereotyping. Noting that Price Waterhouse could avoid equitable relief by proving by clear and convincing evidence that it would have placed Hopkins' candidacy on hold even absent this discrimination, the judge decided that the firm had not carried this heavy burden.

The Court of Appeals affirmed the District Court's ultimate conclusion, but departed from its analysis in one particular: it held that, even if a plaintiff proves that discrimination played a role in an employment decision, the defendant will not be found liable if it proves, by clear and convincing evidence, that it would have made the same decision in the absence of discrimination. Under this approach, an employer is not deemed to have violated Title VII if it proves that it would have made the same decision in the absence of an impermissible motive, whereas, under the District Court's approach, the employer's proof in that respect only avoids equitable relief. We decide today that the Court of Appeals had the better approach, but that both courts erred in requiring the employer to make its proof by clear and convincing evidence.

The Requirements of Title VII

The specification of the standard of causation under Title VII is a decision about the kind of conduct that violates that statute. According to Price Waterhouse, an employer violates Title VII only if it gives decisive consideration to an employee's gender, race, national origin, or religion in making a decision that affects that employee. On Price Waterhouse's theory, even if a plaintiff shows that her gender played a part in an employment decision, it is still her burden to show that the decision would have been different if the employer had not discriminated. In Hopkins' view, on the other hand, an employer violates the statute whenever it allows one of these attributes to play any part in an employment decision. Once a plaintiff shows that this occurred, according to Hopkins, the employer's proof that it would have made the same decision in the absence of discrimination can serve to limit equitable relief, but not to avoid a finding of liability. We conclude that, as often happens, the truth lies somewhere in-between.

In passing Title VII, Congress made the simple but momentous announcement that sex, race, religion, and national origin are not relevant to the selection, evaluation, or compensation of employees. Yet the statute does not purport to limit the other qualities and characteristics that employers may take into account in making employment decisions. The converse, therefore, of "for cause" legislation, Title VII eliminates certain bases for distinguishing among employees while otherwise preserving employers' freedom of choice. This balance between employee rights and employer prerogatives turns out to be decisive in the case before us.

Congress' intent to forbid employers to take gender into account in making employment decisions appears on the face of the statute. In now-familiar language, the statute forbids an employer to

> fail or refuse to hire or to discharge any individual, or otherwise to discriminate with respect to his compensation, terms, conditions, or privileges of employment,

or to

> limit, segregate, or classify his employees or applicants for employment in any way which would deprive or tend to deprive any individual of employment opportunities or otherwise adversely affect his status as an employee, *because of* such individual's . . . sex.

We take these words to mean that gender must be irrelevant to employment decisions. . . .

Sex Stereotyping and Gender Discrimination

In saying that gender played a motivating part in an employment decision, we mean that, if we asked the employer at the moment of the decision what its reasons were and if we received a truthful response, one of those reasons would be that the applicant or employee was a woman. In the specific context of sex stereotyping, an employer who acts on the basis of a belief that a woman cannot be aggressive, or that she must not be, has acted on the basis of gender.

Although the parties do not overtly dispute this last proposition, the placement by Price Waterhouse of "sex stereotyping" in quotation marks throughout its brief seems to us an insinuation either that such stereotyping was not present in this case or that it lacks legal relevance. We reject both possibilities. As to the existence of sex stereotyping in this case, we are not inclined to quarrel with the District Court's conclusion that a number of the partners' comments showed sex stereotyping at work. As for the legal relevance of sex stereotyping, we are beyond the day when an employer could evaluate employees by assuming or insisting that they matched the stereotype associated with their group, for,

> "[i]n forbidding employers to discriminate against individuals because of their sex, Congress intended to strike at the entire spectrum of disparate treatment of men and women resulting from sex stereotypes." [*Los Angeles Dept. of Water & Power v. Manhart* (1978)]

An employer who objects to aggressiveness in women but whose positions require this trait places women in an intolerable and impermissible Catch-22: out of a job if they behave aggressively and out of a job if they do not. Title VII lifts women out of this bind.

Remarks at work that are based on sex stereotypes do not inevitably prove that gender played a part in a particular employment decision. The plaintiff must show that the employer actually relied on her gender in making its decision. In making this showing, stereotyped remarks can certainly be evidence that gender played a part. In any event, the stereotyping in this case did not simply consist of stray remarks. On the contrary, Hopkins proved that Price Waterhouse invited partners to submit comments; that some of the comments stemmed from sex stereotypes; that an important part of the Policy Board's decision on Hopkins was an assessment of the submitted comments; and that Price Waterhouse in no way disclaimed reliance on the sex-linked evaluations. This is not, as Price Waterhouse suggests, "discrimination in the air"; rather, it is, as Hopkins puts it, "discrimination brought to ground and visited upon" an employee. By focusing on Hopkins' specific proof, however, we do not suggest a limitation on the possible ways of proving that stereotyping played a motivating role in an employment decision, and we refrain from deciding here which specific facts, "standing alone," would or would not establish a plaintiff's case, since such a decision is unnecessary in this case.

As to the employer's proof, in most cases, the employer should be able to present some objective evidence as to its probable decision in the absence of an impermissible motive. Moreover, proving "that the same decision would have been justified . . . is not the same as proving that the same decision would have been made" [*Givhan v. Western Line Consolidated School District* (1979)]. An employer may not, in other words, prevail in a mixed-motives case by offering a legitimate and sufficient reason for its decision if that reason did not motivate it at the time of the decision. Finally, an employer may not meet its burden in such a case by merely showing that, at the time of the decision, it was motivated only in part by a legitimate reason. The very premise of a mixed-motives case is that a legitimate reason was present, and indeed, in this case, Price Waterhouse already has made this showing by convincing Judge Gesell that Hopkins' interpersonal problems were a legitimate concern. The employer instead must show that its legitimate reason, standing alone, would have induced it to make the same decision.

Need for Preponderance of Evidence

The courts below held that an employer who has allowed a discriminatory impulse to play a motivating part in an employment decision must prove by clear and convincing evidence that it would have made the same decision in the absence of discrimination. We are persuaded that the better rule is that the employer must make this showing by a preponderance of the evidence. . . .

Although Price Waterhouse does not concretely tell us how its proof was preponderant, even if it was not clear and convincing, this general claim is implicit in its request for the less stringent standard. Since the lower courts required Price Waterhouse to make its proof by clear and convincing evidence, they did not determine whether Price Waterhouse had proved by a preponderance of the evidence that it would have placed Hopkins' candidacy on hold even if it had not permitted sex-linked evaluations to play a part in the decisionmaking process. Thus, we shall remand this case so that that determination can be made.

The District Court found that sex stereotyping "was permitted to play a part" in the evaluation of Hopkins as a candidate for partnership. Price Waterhouse disputes both that stereotyping occurred and that it played any part in the decision to place Hopkins' candidacy on hold. In the firm's view, in other words, the District Court's factual conclusions are clearly erroneous. We do not agree. . . .

It takes no special training to discern sex stereotyping in a description of an aggressive female employee as requiring "a course at charm school." Nor, turning to Thomas Beyer's memorable advice to Hopkins, does it require expertise in psychology to know that, if an employee's flawed "interpersonal skills" can be corrected by a soft-hued suit or a new shade of lipstick, perhaps it is the employee's sex, and not her interpersonal skills, that has drawn the criticism. . . .

Price Waterhouse appears to think that we cannot affirm the factual findings of the trial court without deciding that, instead of being overbearing and aggressive and curt, Hopkins is, in fact, kind and considerate and patient. If this is indeed its impression, petitioner misunderstands the theory on which Hopkins prevailed. The District Judge acknowledged that Hopkins' conduct justified complaints about her behavior as a senior manager. But he also concluded that the reactions of at least some of the partners were reactions to her as a woman manager. Where an evaluation is based on a subjective assessment of a person's strengths and weaknesses, it is simply not true that each evaluator will focus on, or even mention, the same weaknesses. Thus, even if we knew that Hopkins had "personality problems," this would not tell us that the partners who cast their evaluations of Hopkins in sex-based terms would have criticized her as sharply (or criticized her at all) if she had been a man. It is not our job to review the evidence and decide that the negative reactions to Hopkins were based on reality; our perception of Hopkins' character is irrelevant. We sit not to determine whether Ms. Hopkins is nice, but to decide whether the partners reacted negatively to her personality because she is a woman.

We hold that, when a plaintiff in a Title VII case proves that her gender played a motivating part in an employment decision, the defendant may avoid a finding of liability only by proving by a preponderance of the evidence that it would have made the same decision even if it had not taken the plaintiff's gender into account. Because the courts below erred by deciding that the defendant must make this proof by clear and convincing evidence, we reverse the Court of Appeals' judgment against Price Waterhouse on liability and remand the case to that court for further proceedings.

Dissenting Opinion: The Burden of Proof to Show Sex Discrimination Should Remain with the Employee

Anthony Kennedy

Anthony Kennedy was appointed to the U.S. Supreme Court by President Ronald Reagan in 1988. Since the retirement of Justice Sandra Day O'Connor in 2006, Kennedy is often considered to be the swing vote on the Court, sometimes taking a liberal position and at other times a more conservative stance.

In the following excerpt from Kennedy's dissent in the 1989 case of Price Waterhouse v. Hopkins, *Kennedy expresses his disagreement with the Court's decision. He believes that the Court goes too far in shifting the burden of proof to the employer if a plaintiff shows that gender played a part in an employment decision, allowing the employer to avoid liability only if it can show by a preponderance of the evidence that it would have made the same decision without considering gender. Kennedy argues that the previous precedent for Title VII discrimination cases, which placed the burden of proof on the employee to prove the existence of discrimination, was more practical and less confusing than the new standard that shifts the burden of proof in*

Anthony Kennedy, dissenting opinion, *Price Waterhouse v. Hopkins*, U.S. Supreme Court, May 1, 1989.

some cases. He concludes that sex stereotyping by employers in employment decisions does not always indicate sex discrimination and says he believes that in this case sex discrimination was not proven.

Today the Court manipulates existing and complex rules for employment discrimination cases in a way certain to result in confusion. Continued adherence to the evidentiary scheme established in *McDonnell Douglas Corp. v. Green*, (1973), and *Texas Dept. of Community Affairs v. Burdine* (1981), is a wiser course than creation of more disarray in an area of the law already difficult for the bench and bar, and so I must dissent.

The Court's Decision

Before turning to my reasons for disagreement with the Court's disposition of the case, it is important to review the actual holding of today's decision. I read the opinions as establishing that, in a limited number of cases Title VII plaintiffs, by presenting direct and substantial evidence of discriminatory animus [hostility], may shift the burden of persuasion to the defendant to show that an adverse employment decision would have been supported by legitimate reasons. The shift in the burden of persuasion occurs only where a plaintiff proves by direct evidence that an unlawful motive was a substantial factor actually relied upon in making the decision. As the opinions make plain, the evidentiary scheme created today is not for every case in which a plaintiff produces evidence of stray remarks in the workplace.

Where the plaintiff makes the requisite showing, the burden that shifts to the employer is to show that legitimate employment considerations would have justified the decision without reference to any impermissible motive. The employer's proof on the point is to be presented and reviewed just as with any other evidentiary question: the Court does not accept the plurality's suggestion that an employer's evidence need be "objective" or otherwise out of the ordinary.

In sum, the Court alters the evidentiary framework of *McDonnell Douglas* and *Burdine* for a closely defined set of cases. Although Justice [Sandra Day] O'Connor advances some thoughtful arguments for this change, I remain convinced that it is unnecessary and unwise. More troubling is the plurality's rationale for today's decision, which includes a number of unfortunate pronouncements on both causation and methods of proof in employment discrimination cases. To demonstrate the defects in the plurality's reasoning, it is necessary to discuss, first, the standard of causation in Title VII cases, and, second, the burden of proof.

The Standard of Causation

The plurality describes this as a case about the standard of causation under Title VII, but I respectfully suggest that the description is misleading. Much of the plurality's rhetoric is spent denouncing a "but-for" standard of causation. The theory of Title VII liability the plurality adopts, however, essentially incorporates the but-for standard. The importance of today's decision is not the standard of causation it employs, but its shift to the defendant of the burden of proof. The plurality's causation analysis is misdirected, for it is clear that, whoever bears the burden of proof on the issue, Title VII liability requires a finding of but-for causation.

The words of Title VII are not obscure. The part of the statute relevant to this case provides:

> It shall be an unlawful employment practice for an employer—
>
> (1) to fail or refuse to hire or to discharge any individual, or otherwise to discriminate against any individual with respect to his compensation, terms, conditions, or privileges of employment, *because of* such individual's race, color, religion, sex, or national origin [emphasis added].

By any normal understanding, the phrase "because of" conveys the idea that the motive in question made a difference to the outcome. We use the words this way in everyday speech. And assuming, as the plurality does, that we ought to consider the interpretive memorandum prepared by the statute's drafters, we find that this is what the words meant to them as well. "To discriminate is to make a distinction, to make a difference in treatment or favor." Congress could not have chosen a clearer way to indicate that proof of liability under Title VII requires a showing that race, color, religion, sex, or national origin caused the decision at issue.

Our decisions confirm that Title VII is not concerned with the mere presence of impermissible motives; it is directed to employment decisions that result from those motives. . . .

An Internal Inconsistency

The most confusing aspect of the plurality's analysis of causation and liability is its internal inconsistency. The plurality begins by saying:

> When . . . an employer considers both gender and legitimate factors at the time of making a decision: that decision was "because of" sex and the other, legitimate considerations— even if we may say later, in the context of litigation, that the decision would have been the same if gender had not been taken into account.

Yet it goes on to state that

> an employer shall not be liable if it can prove that, even if it had not taken gender into account, it would have come to the same decision.

Given the language of the statute, these statements cannot both be true. Title VII unambiguously states that an employer who makes decisions "because of" sex has violated the statute. The plurality's first statement therefore appears to indicate that an employer who considers illegitimate reasons when making a decision is a violator. But the opinion then tells us that the employer who shows that the same decision would have been made absent consideration of sex is not a violator. If the second statement is to be reconciled with the language of Title VII, it must be that a decision that would have been the same absent consideration of sex was not made "because of" sex. In other words, there is no violation of the statute absent but-for causation. The plurality's description of the "same decision" test it adopts supports this view. The opinion states that

> [a] court that finds for a plaintiff under this standard has effectively concluded that an illegitimate motive was a "but-for" cause of the employment decision,

and that this "is not an imposition of liability 'where sex made no difference to the outcome.'"

The plurality attempts to reconcile its internal inconsistency on the causation issue by describing the employer's showing as an "affirmative defense." This is nothing more than a label, and one not round in the language or legislative history of Title VII. . . . The import of today's decision is not that Title VII liability can arise without but-for causation, but that, in certain cases, it is not the plaintiff who must prove the presence of causation, but the defendant who must prove its absence.

The Burden of Proof

We established the order of proof for individual Title VII disparate treatment cases in *McDonnell Douglas*, and reaffirmed this allocation in *Burdine*. Under *Burdine*, once the plaintiff presents a *prima facie* [apparent] case, an inference of discrimination arises. The employer must rebut the inference by articulating a legitimate nondiscriminatory reason for its action. The final burden of persuasion, however, belongs to the plaintiff. *Burdine* makes clear that the ultimate burden of persuading the trier of fact that the defendant intentionally discriminated against the plaintiff remains at all times with the plaintiff.

I would adhere to this established evidentiary framework, which provides the appropriate standard for this and other individual disparate treatment cases. Today's creation of a new set of rules for "mixed-motives" cases is not mandated by the statute itself. The Court's attempt at refinement provides limited practical benefits at the cost of confusion and complexity, with the attendant risk that the trier of fact will misapprehend the controlling legal principles and reach an incorrect decision. . . .

The potential benefits of the new approach, in my view, are overstated. First, the Court makes clear that the *Price Waterhouse* scheme is applicable only in those cases where the plaintiff has produced direct and substantial proof that an impermissible motive was relied upon in making the decision at issue. The burden shift properly will be found to apply in only a limited number of employment discrimination cases. The application of the new scheme, furthermore, will make a difference only in a smaller subset of cases. The practical importance of the burden of proof is the "risk of nonpersuasion," and the new system will make a difference only where the evidence is so evenly balanced that the factfinder cannot say that either side's explanation of the case is "more likely" true. This category will not include cases in which the allocation of the burden of proof will be dispositive because of a complete lack of evidence on the causation issue. Rather, *Price Waterhouse* will apply only to cases in which there is substantial evidence of reliance on an impermissible motive, as well as evidence from the employer that legitimate reasons supported its action.

Although the *Price Waterhouse* system is not for every case, almost every plaintiff is certain to ask for a *Price Waterhouse* instruction, perhaps on the basis of "stray remarks" or other evidence of discriminatory animus. Trial and appellate courts will therefore be saddled with the task of developing standards for determining when to apply the burden shift. One of their new tasks will be the generation of a jurisprudence of the meaning of "substantial factor." Courts will also be required to make the often subtle and difficult distinction between "direct" and "indirect" or "circumstantial" evidence. Lower courts long have had difficulty applying *McDonnell Douglas* and *Burdine*. Addition of a second burden-shifting mechanism, the application of which itself depends on assessment of credibility and a determination whether evidence is sufficiently direct and substantial, is not likely to lend clarity to the process. . . .

Sex Stereotyping and Discrimination

The ultimate question in every individual disparate treatment case is whether discrimination caused the particular decision at issue. Some of the plurality's comments with respect to the District Court's findings in this case, however, are potentially misleading. As the plurality notes, the District Court based its liability determination on expert evidence that some evaluations of respondent Hopkins were based on unconscious sex stereotypes, and on the fact that Price Waterhouse failed to disclaim reliance on these comments when it conducted the partnership review. The District Court also based liability on Price Waterhouse's failure to

> make partners sensitive to the dangers [of stereotyping], to discourage comments tainted by sexism, or to investigate comments to determine whether they were influenced by stereotypes.

Although the District Court's version of Title VII liability is improper under any of today's opinions, I think it important to stress that Title VII creates no independent cause of action for sex stereotyping. Evidence of use by decisionmakers of sex stereotypes is, of course, quite relevant to the question of discriminatory intent. The ultimate question, however, is whether discrimination caused the plaintiff's harm. Our cases do not support the suggestion that failure to "disclaim reliance" on stereotypical comments itself violates Title VII. Neither do they support creation of a "duty to sensitize." As the dissenting judge in the Court of Appeals observed, acceptance of such theories would turn Title VII "from a prohibition of discriminatory conduct into an engine for rooting out sexist thoughts."

Employment discrimination claims require factfinders to make difficult and sensitive decisions. Sometimes this may mean that no finding of discrimination is justified even though a qualified employee is passed over by a less than admirable employer. In other cases, Title VII's protections properly extend to plaintiffs who are by no means model employees. As Justice [William J.] Brennan notes, courts do not sit to determine whether litigants are nice. In this case, Hopkins plainly presented a strong case both of her own professional qualifications and of the presence of discrimination in Price Waterhouse's partnership process. Had the District Court found on this record that sex discrimination caused the adverse decision, I doubt it would have been reversible error. That decision was for the finder of fact, however, and the District Court made plain that sex discrimination was not a but-for cause of the decision to place Hopkins' partnership candidacy on hold. Attempts to evade tough decisions by erecting novel theories of liability or multitiered systems of shifting burdens are misguided.

The language of Title VII and our well considered precedents require this plaintiff to establish that the decision to place her candidacy on hold was made "because of" sex. Here the District Court found that the "comments of the individual partners and the expert evidence ... do not prove an intentional discriminatory motive or purpose," and that,

> [b]ecause plaintiff has considerable problems dealing with staff and peers, the Court cannot say that she would have been elected to partnership if the Policy Board's decision had not been tainted by sexually based evaluations,

Hopkins thus failed to meet the requisite standard of proof after a full trial. I would remand the case for entry of judgment in favor of Price Waterhouse.

"The case law seems to establish a relatively low threshold for a trial court to place the ultimate burden of proof on the employer."

Employer Burden of Proof in Discrimination Cases Has Expanded Since *Price Waterhouse*

Jonathan I. Nirenberg

Jonathan I. Nirenberg is an attorney in New Jersey specializing in discrimination, civil rights, and other employment law cases.

In the following article, Nirenberg recounts the development of case law in the area of employment discrimination. He explains how the Supreme Court's decision in Price Waterhouse v. Hopkins, *wherein the Court determined that in certain cases the burden of proof shifts to the employer to disprove discrimination, expanded the previous understanding of discrimination under Title VII that had placed the burden of proof on the employee to prove discrimination. Nirenberg claims that since* Price Waterhouse, *the understanding of discrimination under Title VII within the courts has shifted even further in favor of the employee, placing a greater burden of proof on employers to disprove discrimination in the face of evidence supporting a discrimination claim.*

U ntil relatively recently, a plaintiff seeking to prove intentional discrimination always had the ultimate burden to prove the discrimination. However, in 1989 that began to change. Initially, the ultimate burden shifted to defendants in cases in which the employer admitted it considered a discriminatory reason for the adverse employment action. But more recently courts have begun placing the ultimate burden of proof on the employer in cases in which the evidence falls short of an admission. Unfortunately, with limited case law on the subject, there is little guidance with respect to when the burden of proof should fall on the employer, rather than the employee. However, the cases seem to indicate that the ultimate burden should be on the employer when the plaintiff presents some evidence of discriminatory animus by the decision-maker.

The *McDonnell Douglas* Test

In 1968, in the landmark decision of *McDonnell Douglas Corp. v. Green* 411 U.S. 792 (1973), the United States Supreme court held that the ultimate burden of proof in a discrimination case is on the plaintiff. The Supreme Court established a three-step burden-shifting test to prove discrimination, starting with the plaintiff proving a *prima facie* case of discrimination. Establishing a prima facie creates an inference of discrimination, and shifts the burden of production to the defendant to articulate a nondiscriminatory legitimate business reason for its action. If the defendant meets this limited burden, then the plaintiff has the ultimate burden to prove that discrimination was a determinative factor in the defendant's action. Although *McDonnell Douglas* itself was a race discrimination case decided under Title VII, courts have applied its "determinative factor" test to virtually all forms of discrimination cases. See, e.g., *Lawrence v. National Westminster Bank New Jersey*, 98 F.3d 61, 69 (3d. Cir. 1996) (recognizing *McDonnell Douglas* test applies to case under the ADA and the ADEA); *Peper v.*

Princeton Universit Bd. of Trustees, 77 N.J. 55, 82 (1978) (applying *McDonnell Douglas* test to case under the New Jersey Law Against Discrimination).

Since direct evidence of discrimination is difficult to come by, one of the more common ways for a plaintiff to meet its ultimate burden of proof under *McDonnell Douglas* is through evidence of pretext, meaning evidence suggesting the employer's explanation for taking the adverse employment action is false. *Bergen Commercial Bank v. Sisler*, 157 N.J. 188, 209-10 (1999). In many cases, evidence of pretext, combined with the elements of the prima facie case, is sufficient to prove intentional discrimination. *Reeves v. Sanderson Plumbing Products, Inc.*, 530 U.S. 133, 147 (2000).

The Mixed-Motive Test

In 1989, the United States Supreme Court recognized that it does not make sense to apply the *McDonnell Douglas* test in cases in which the employer admits it had a discriminatory reason for an adverse employment actions, but claims it would have made the same decision even if it had not considered the discriminatory reason. *Price Waterhouse v. Hopkins*, 490 U.S. 228 (1989). Thus, in a "mixed motive" case, once the plaintiff proves a prima facie case the burden shifts to the employer to prove it would have made the same decision even irrespective of its discriminatory reason.

More recent cases have recognized that the mixed-motive test applies to cases in which the employer does not admit it considered a discriminatory factor. For example, the New Jersey Supreme Court has interpreted the phrase "direct evidence" in the context of the mixed-motive proof pattern to include circumstantial evidence that "directly reflects" the alleged discriminatory animus. *McDevitt v. Bill Good Builders, Inc.*, 175 N.J. 519, 528-529 (2003); *Fleming v. Corr. Healthcare Solutions, Inc.*, 164 N.J. 90 (2000).

Extending the mixed-motive test even further, in *Desert Palace, Inc. v. Costa*, the United States Supreme Court held that direct evidence is not required to invoke the mixed-motive test, but rather the ultimate burden of proof is on the employer if the plaintiff presents sufficient evidence for a reasonable jury to conclude that a discriminatory factor was a motivating factor in the employer's decision to take the adverse employment action. *Desert Palace, Inc. v. Costa* 539 U.S. 90, 101 (2003).

Specifically, the Supreme Court allowed a mixed-motive jury charge based on the plaintiff's evidence that she was the only female employee working in the defendant's warehouse, and her supervisor singled her out, gave her harsher discipline than her male co-workers, assigned her less overtime than her male counterparts, repeatedly "stacked" her disciplinary record, and either used or tolerated sex-based slurs against her.

In holding that the mixed-motive test applies even though there was no direct evidence of discrimination, the Supreme Court relied on a 1991 amendment to Title VII, as well as other factors including the fact that circumstantial evidence can often be just as powerful as direct evidence. However, it did not provide clear guidance to trial courts with respect to when they should place the ultimate burden of proof of the employer.

The Burden of Proof

Two years later, in *Myers v. AT&T Corp* the Appellate Division adopted *Desert Palace* under New Jersey law, holding that direct evidence is not required for the mixed-motive proof pattern to apply. *Myers v. AT&T*, 300 N.J. Super. 443, 452 (App. Div. 2005), *certif. denied*, 186 N.J. 244 (2006). Ultimately, when it applied the law to the facts of the case, the Appellate Division found there was direct evidence of disability discrimination as there was an admission by the plaintiff's supervisor that she lowered the plaintiff's performance rating because she perceived that, as a cancer survivor, the plaintiff was not working as hard as her nondisabled coworker, leading the employer to select the plaintiff for a layoff. Given this direct evidence, the Court did not need to consider the limits of *Desert Palace*'s holding.

Despite the lack of express guidance on when the burden of proof should be on the employer, the case law seems to establish a relatively low threshold for a trial court to place the ultimate burden of proof on the employer. Specifically, *Myers* indicates that the focus should be on the plaintiff's evidence when there is a factual dispute. Likewise, while there may need to be some evidence of discriminatory animus, based on its facts, *Desert Palace* suggest that the evidence does not have to directly relate to the adverse employment action at issue in the litigation. Thus, while more guidance from appellate courts undeniably would be helpful, it appears that the ultimate burden of proof should be on the employer if the evidence of discrimination is more than the evidence supporting the prima-facie case and evidence of pretext.

"Courts appear to have concluded that one can directly infer the existence of discrimination from the existence of stereotypes."

Price Waterhouse Rests on an Unwarranted Suspicion of Stereotypes

Barbara B. Brown, Neal D. Mollen, and Erica Larsen

Barbara B. Brown, Neal D. Mollen, and Erica Larsen are attorneys at a firm specializing in employment law.

In the following article, Brown, Mollen, and Larsen contend that courts have made too much of the link between stereotypes and discrimination. They claim that this link was first established in Price Waterhouse v. Hopkins, *in which the Supreme Court determined that an employer's use of gender stereotypes in an employment decision creates a strong presumption of discrimination, shifting the burden of proof to the employer to prove the stereotyping did not influence the employment decision. Brown, Mollen, and Larsen claim that research about stereotypes does not support the view that the existence of stereotypes results in discrimination and, furthermore, that there is some truth behind stereotypes that should mitigate a presumption of bias on the part of someone using stereotypes.*

Barbara B. Brown, Neal D. Mollen, and Erica Larsen, "The Limits of Stereotypes," *Legal Times*, vol. 28, February 21, 2005. Multiple subheads inserted for clarity. Copyright © 2005 ALM Properties, LLC. As of 2009 Legal Times is part of The National Law Journal. All rights reserved. Further duplication without permission is prohibited. Reproduced by permission.

Close your eyes and imagine someone baking brownies in a country kitchen. The baker you conjure is likely to look more like Aunt Bea than, say, Ice-T. If you are asked to visualize "a terrorist," the resulting mental image is far more likely to look like Mohamed Atta than Madeleine Albright.

Generalizations About Groups

Are these mental images the product of an intractable discriminatory mind-set—latent internalized stereotypes—or does the human brain innocently (and sensibly) supply these images by playing the odds? And does this phenomenon have any necessary implication for how employers judge individuals in the employment setting?

There can be no doubt that it is unlawful to rely on generalizations to deny an individual an employment opportunity, even if the generalization is accurate for the group as a whole. In *City of Los Angeles, Department of Water & Power v. Manhart* (1978), the Supreme Court observed that "employment decisions cannot be predicated on mere 'stereotyped' impressions about the characteristics of males or females. Myths and purely habitual assumptions about a woman's inability to perform certain kinds of work are no longer acceptable reasons for refusing to employ qualified individuals, or for paying them less."

Thus, as this case noted, "[i]f height is required for a job, a tall woman may not be refused employment merely because, on the average, women are too short. Even a true generalization about the class is an insufficient reason for disqualifying an individual to whom the generalization does not apply."

Accordingly, employers must ensure that they are basing employment decisions on the attributes of each individual worker, and not on the perceived attributes of the class to which he or she belongs.

Stereotypes and Discrimination

Stereotypes as a legal concept gained greater currency as a result of *Price Waterhouse v. Hopkins* (1989). In that Supreme Court case, the plaintiff accused the accounting firm of denying her a partnership because of her gender.

The firm had criticized the female plaintiff for her "aggressiveness," when that trait was valued in males. Female candidates for partnership, the Court observed, were "viewed favorably if partners believed they maintained their femininity while becoming effective professional managers," a standard that, by definition, was never applied to males. The Court found evidence of bias in the fact that one of the partners had urged the plaintiff to "walk more femininely, talk more femininely, dress more femininely, wear makeup, have her hair styled, and wear jewelry."

More recently, the Supreme Court has upheld Congress' decision to entitle all employees, male and female, to unpaid leave in order to prevent women from being fired for excessive absenteeism when they conform to the stereotype of being overwhelmingly the ones who take time off to care for others. In *Nevada Department of Human Resources v. Hibbs* (2003), the Court observed that the Family and Medical Leave Act was Congress' effort to address "the fault line between work and family—precisely where sex-based *overgeneralization* has been and remains strongest" (emphasis added).

As these cases affirm, federal laws against employment discrimination forcefully reject the idea that every member of a demographic group can be assumed to possess the characteristics that many of those in the group possess. But after *Price Waterhouse*, the lower courts began to turn that simple employment principle into a cause of action.

These courts appear to have concluded that one can directly infer the existence of discrimination from the existence of stereotypes. This concept has complicated and misdirected employment law.

Research About Stereotypes

But the greatest problem arises where the concept of stereotyping invades class action law. Class actions are being built upon the assertion that managers harbor, and inevitably rely upon, racial and gender stereotypes in making employment decisions. And that reliance supposedly explains statistical imbalances.

Plaintiffs have begun to place central reliance on the testimony of social scientists willing to assign differences in employment results to the operation of stereotypes. That testimony has been accepted uncritically by courts as potent evidence of classwide injury, but the data simply do not support the conclusions offered.

Although there is a significant body of scientific literature in the field of stereotypes, that work consists almost entirely of studies performed on campus, with students (working for extra credit) as the subjects. These subjects are asked, for example, to screen résumés of fictitious job applicants with obviously male, female, or gender-ambiguous names (or names supposedly typical of other demographic groups).

But the laboratory is not the real world, and most professionals doing serious research in this field of study warn about the limited "external validity" of these studies—the power of the studies to predict human behavior in settings infinitely more complex than the laboratory.

Even in the laboratory, this research shows, sensibly enough, that decisionmaking based on stereotypes is most likely to occur when the decision-maker knows little or nothing about the "target" other than that specific demographic information.

If you were asked to choose a team for a game of football, and you had no further information about the individuals from whom to select players other than gender, it might well be sensible to pick all males based on the assumption that men are more interested in and more experienced at playing the sport than women.

But if you could actually see these individuals, you might well decide to select certain young, athletic females instead of bedraggled, graying, potbellied male employment lawyers. That is, you would rely on the actual data you had at hand—called "individuating information" in the field of stereotype research—rather than the group generalizations with which you might have begun the process.

Similarly, when a manager decides to promote an individual or hand out bonuses, the manager has a rich source of "individuating" information—observed employee performance—on which to base a decision, and, as the research shows, is far less likely to rely on stereotypes.

The Truth Behind Stereotypes

The mischief posed by the stereotype research for employers arises because employment law proof schemes have traditionally treated any difference in outcomes among demographic groups as prima facie evidence of bias.

Only the bravest of employers would dare offer as an explanation for such a perceived imbalance the explanation that men and women (or different racial or ethnic groups) differ meaningfully with respect to, say, interest in particular types of employment. As a result, plaintiffs often have free rein to argue, with the aid of "expert" testimony and judicial abdication of enforcement of the rules for admitting expert testimony, that the imbalance exists because of managerial reliance on stereotypes operating at the subconscious level.

But the truth is that many (though certainly not all) stereotypes have a basis in fact. An "imbalance" that is consistent with a commonly held stereotype is not necessarily, or even likely, caused by the employer's reliance on that stereotype. Instead, it may well be caused by the facts that underlie the stereotype.

Empirical data, from study after study, show that as a group, women in this country do shoulder a disproportionate share of the workload in the home, have disproportionate responsibilities for child care and household maintenance, and thus as a group are proportionately less interested than men in jobs with unpredictable schedules or the need to relocate. College enrollment statistics unequivocally show that men, women, and various ethnic and racial groups are attracted to various fields of study at different rates.

The Presumption of Bias

One frequent assertion made by plaintiffs' experts in the area is that managers in an environment dominated by a particular group (typically white males) tend to disregard or discount the accomplishments of "out-group" workers—that minority group members do not get proper credit for their achievements because of the pernicious effect of stereotypes. But in a study of women in various law schools with relatively larger and smaller female populations, researchers with the University of Massachusetts and the American Bar Foundation found that it was the behavior of the female students—not their male professors—that varied depending on the size of the female population.

Specifically, the study found that the actual performance of women on anonymously graded exams rose with the percentage of females in the student population. The finding has profound implications for the importance of affirmative action to be sure, but it also significantly undermines the notion that observed disparities between men and women (and, presumably, among other demographic groups) necessarily arise because of managerial bias.

The question, then, is whether there is any reason to suspect that a particular observed "imbalance" results from pervasive bias rather than material differences between groups of people.

When women get less generous bonuses than men in a largely male work environment, is it because of stereotypical thinking by managers or depressed performance of women? When a computer company's successful software engineers are almost all white and male, is that because hiring managers cannot "see" minorities and women in those roles, or does it reflect something about the interests of people in those groups?

Class action discrimination cases are proliferating in no small measure because courts have been willing to assume a critical role for stereotypes in employment decision making, yet unwilling to consider head-on the available evidence on the very real differences between various demographic groups that can account for differing success rates.

The law of employment discrimination has always been premised on the assumption that interest and ability are equally distributed among men and women and all racial and ethnic groups. Because we have assumed this to be true, we expect to find at least rough parity of outcomes among all of these groups. When we do not see such parity, the law imposes a presumption that the employer has relied upon some unlawful characteristic to account for the shortfall.

There is sufficient evidence in the social science literature to question the viability of this assumption.

I *"In many respects, breaking stereotypes
is about eliminating assumptions."*

The Need to Combat Sex Stereotyping After *Price Waterhouse* Still Exists

Jonathan A. Segal

Jonathan A. Segal is an employment lawyer and managing principal of the Duane Morris Institute, which provides training workshops for professionals focused on employment issues faced by managers and administrators.

In the following selection, Segal contends that gender stereotyping still exists in many forms. He claims that the legal significance of gender stereotyping was established by the U.S. Supreme Court's decision in Price Waterhouse v. Hopkins, *wherein the Court determined that an employer's use of gender stereotypes in making employment decisions creates an assumption of discrimination without a preponderance of the evidence showing otherwise. Segal claims that the sort of stereotyping at issue in* Price Waterhouse *is not as common today, but that women continue to face a difficult situation in leadership positions because they are female. Additionally, Segal claims that stereotypes about working mothers, and even positive stereotypes, are common as forms of discrimination against women.*

As we all know, Title VII of the Civil Rights Act of 1964 prohibits discrimination on account of sex, race, color,

Jonathan A. Segal, "Woman in the Moon: Gender Stereotypes Are Not a Thing of the Past, and Will Be Reflected in the Future of Employment Law Litigation," *HR Magazine*, vol. 52, August 2007, pp. 107–108, 110, 112–14. Copyright © Society for Human Resource Management 2007. Reproduced by permission.

religion and national origin. Too often, though, managers fail to grasp that Title VII's mandate bars employers from acting on gender stereotypes.

In 1989, the U.S. Supreme Court held that an employer may be guilty of engaging in unlawful sex discrimination, even if the employer does not directly consider gender but rather relies on gender stereotypes about the individual. At the time, the decision was heralded as groundbreaking. Today, it is hard to imagine any other outcome. . . .

Legal Significance of Stereotyping

In *Price Waterhouse v. Hopkins* (1989), the key issue was whether Ann Hopkins was denied partnership because of her sex.

From the record, it appears that there was no question that she was intellectually capable and very successful in terms of client relations and business generation. To quote the district court judge, she "was generally viewed as a highly competent project leader who worked long hours, pushed vigorously to meet deadlines and demanded much from the multidisciplinary staffs."

However, Hopkins' pushing hard may have been too much of a good thing. According to the district court, both "supporters and opponents of her candidacy indicated that she was sometimes overly aggressive, unduly harsh, difficult to work with and impatient with staff."

These were undeniably legitimate concerns. However, there also were indications that some of the negative reaction to Hopkins' behavior may have been attributable to her gender. One partner described her as macho. Another suggested that she overcompensated for being a woman. A third recommended that she take a course at charm school.

And one of the key decision-makers told her that, to improve her chances for partnership, Hopkins should "walk more femininely, wear make-up, have her hair styled and wear jewelry."

The Supreme Court agreed with the district court that Price Waterhouse had legitimate reasons to deny Hopkins partnership in light of some of the problems with her interpersonal style. But the Supreme Court also agreed with the district court that some of the comments made about Hopkins were based on a stereotypic view of what is acceptable behavior for a woman.

As for the legal significance of gender stereotyping, the Supreme Court stated "we are beyond the day when an employer can evaluate employees by assuming or insisting that they match the stereotypes associated with their group. . . . An employer who objects to aggressiveness in women but whose positions require this trait place women in an intolerable Catch-22: out of a job if they behave aggressively and out of a job if they do not. Title VII lifts women out of this bind."

A Real Catch-22

In light of increased sensitivity to gender stereotyping and management training, it is not likely that knuckle-dragging comments of the kind made in *Hopkins* would be repeated today in most responsible companies. However, that does not mean that gender stereotypes are a thing of the past.

The Catch-22 aptly described in *Hopkins* remains a real obstacle for women in leadership positions. If a woman is direct and assertive, she may get branded with a scarlet "B." If she is more indirect and collaborative, she may be dismissed as nice but ineffective.

This very real Catch-22 contributes to the glass ceiling that still exists in many organizations. To borrow from pop culture, Donald Trump is often praised as being "in control," while Martha Stewart is blasted as being "controlling." . . .

The Maternal Wall

Gender stereotyping is not limited to evaluating assertiveness or aggressiveness. It also may apply to a subgroup of women—working women with children. The Equal Employment Opportunity Commission (EEOC) highlighted its concern for gender stereotyping against caregivers, including women with children, in a highly publicized guidance issued on May 23 [2007].

By way of background, the Supreme Court has long recognized a form of discrimination known as "sex-plus" discrimination. That occurs where a person is subject to disparate treatment based not solely on her or his sex, but rather her or his sex in relation to another characteristic, such as marital status or parental status.

In *Phillips v. Martin Marietta Corp.* (1971), the employer refused to hire women with preschool-aged children while the employer would hire men with preschool-aged children. In holding that the employee stated a viable cause of action for sex discrimination, the Supreme Court dismissed the argument that there could be no Title VII violation simply because not all women were affected by the policy.

Instead, the court held that Title VII prohibited the use of "one hiring policy for women and another for men."

Of course, today, responsible employers don't have separate policies for women and men with young children. But just as conscious and unconscious stereotypes about the roles of women may affect how women are evaluated in terms of their leadership style, so may conscious or unconscious stereotypes about the impact of children on a woman's ability to perform at work affect the woman's opportunities.

A case out of the 2nd Circuit is instructive. In *Back v. Hastings on Hudson Union Free School District* (2004), a school psychologist was denied tenure. The school claimed that she was terminated because she lacked the requisite organizational tools and interpersonal skills. In contrast, she claimed that these reasons were a pretext and that the real reason was because the employer assumed that she could not maintain the necessary devotion to her job and be a good mother at the same time.

There were some smoking gun allegations. For example, the employee alleged that the employer not only asked her to plan on spacing her offspring but also expressed concern that a mother with tenure and young children might not show the necessary level of commitment and devotion to her job.

The court correctly stated that "just as it takes no special training to discern sex stereotyping in a description of an aggressive female as requiring a course at charm school . . . so it takes no special training to discern stereotyping in the view that a woman cannot be a 'good mother' and have a job that requires long hours."

Significantly, the employee in *Back* offered no evidence of how men with children were treated. While the court suggested such evidence could have made the employee's case even stronger, its absence was not fatal. In other words, there can be discrimination based on sex (or sex-plus) even without showing a comparator who was treated more favorably. . . .

Positive Stereotypes

To counter these negative stereotypes, sometimes we sell positive stereotypes. For example, in the context of gender, the "benign" stereotype we are most likely to hear is that women actually may be stronger than men in terms of interpersonal skills.

Even if well intended, such benign stereotypes are problematic.

As an initial matter, saying that women are interpersonally stronger than men may serve as the factual predicate for a gender bias claim by a man in a position requiring strong interpersonal skills. One area in which men may suffer from gender-biased stereotypes is in their ability to be nurturing and form strong relationships.

Second, to the extent we generalize that women have a certain skill set, there may be a negative implication that they do not have another critical skill set. Another way of saying someone is interpersonally stronger is to say that they are more sensitive. It is not a difficult leap to go from "more sensitive" to "too sensitive" for line positions.

Finally, saying that women are stronger than men interpersonally means that women who are equal to men on this criterion may actually seem weaker than men.

It's good to sell the values of diversity as a legal and business matter. However, in the process of selling diversity, we need to be careful that we do not stereotype in the name of sensitizing and create higher standards for those we are purporting to help.

Undoubtedly, in some cases, gender stereotyping reflects hostility. To deny misogyny [hatred of women] is to deny reality.

In other cases, it is more a product of ignorance and surprise. Some react differently to women in power, not because they dislike the idea of women having power, but because seeing women in power is relatively new to them.

In many respects, breaking stereotypes is about eliminating assumptions. It means taking a fresh look at how we view the world.

That's why, whenever we talk about the man in the moon, she smiles.

CHAPTER 3

Finding Virginia Military Institute's Single-Sex Policy Unconstitutional

Case Overview

United States v. Virginia (1996)

In *United States v. Virginia*, the U.S. Supreme Court ruled that it was unconstitutional for the Commonwealth of Virginia to fund the Virginia Military Institute, or VMI, because of the institute's exclusion of women. VMI is a public college in Virginia founded in 1839 that had always been a male-only military school. After a female high school student complained in 1990 to the U.S. Department of Justice about VMI's male-only policy, the United States filed a case against Virginia, accusing the state of violating the equal protection clause of the Fourteenth Amendment. The clause guarantees that "no state shall . . . deny to any person within its jurisdiction the equal protection of the laws."

The federal court that first heard the case upheld the male-only admission policy as constitutional, determining that the state had an interest in offering a military-style education in a male-only setting. The U.S. Department of Justice then appealed the case to the U.S. Court of Appeals for the Fourth Circuit. The circuit court determined that the male-only admission policy violated the equal protection clause, advising Virginia to admit women, open a separate military school for women, or stop funding VMI. Virginia responded by creating the Virginia Women's Institute for Leadership (VWIL), a female-only program at Mary Baldwin College in Virginia, modeled on the program at VMI. The circuit court approved the creation of the separate program as satisfying the requirements of the equal protection clause. The U.S. Department of Justice then appealed the case to the U.S. Supreme Court.

Writing for the Court's 7-1 majority, Ruth Bader Ginsburg found that Virginia failed to show a persuasive reason for excluding women. The Court rejected Virginia's proposed alternative, VWIL, because the academy was unlikely to ever equal the quality of the existing institute. The Court also rejected the state's purported interest in the male-only admission policy, determining that there was no substantial interest in excluding women in order to meet the goal of providing citizens of Virginia with a military education. Ginsburg reiterated the standard from a previous case that an "exceedingly persuasive justification" was needed for a state to use public money to treat women differently from men. In this case, the Court concluded that there was no such justification, ordering VMI to accept women.

In August 1997, VMI enrolled its first female cadets, with 30 women joining the class of 2001. As of August 2009, 158 women had graduated from VMI, and there were 129 female cadets enrolled. VMI was the last military college to admit women. Since the decision in *United States v. Virginia*, single-sex education in the public sector is constitutional only if comparable courses, services, and facilities are available to both sexes. Single-sex education still exists at all levels of education, including a handful of female-only public colleges. Single-sex education in primary and secondary school has actually grown since the *Virginia* decision. Private women's colleges and men's colleges are not affected by the decision in *Virginia*, and many small, single-sex colleges still exist. There is debate, however, on whether future Court decisions could challenge the existence of single-sex education altogether.

> "Virginia has shown no 'exceedingly per-
> suasive justification' for excluding all
> women from the citizen soldier train-
> ing afforded by VMI."

Majority Opinion: The All-Male Policy at Virginia Military Institute Is Unconstitutional

Ruth Bader Ginsburg

Ruth Bader Ginsburg was appointed to the Supreme Court in 1993 by President Bill Clinton. She is the second female justice and the first Jewish woman to serve on the Court.

The following is excerpted from Ginsburg's majority opinion in the Supreme Court's 1996 case of United States v. Virginia, *in which it was determined that the male-only admission policy of the Virginia Military Institute (VMI) was in violation of the Fourteenth Amendment by denying women equal protection under the law. The United States sued the Commonwealth of Virginia for violating the equal protection clause of the Fourteenth Amendment by refusing women admission to VMI. The district court denied unconstitutionality, but on appeal, the court of appeals reversed this decision, finding that the male-only policy denied women equal protection. In response, Virginia developed a parallel women's program, Virginia Women's Institute for Leadership (VWIL). The court of appeals accepted the parallel program as satisfying the equal protection requirement. Upon appeal, the Supreme Court determined that the male-only policy of*

Ruth Bader Ginsburg, majority opinion, *United States v. Virginia*, U.S. Supreme Court, June 26, 1996.

VMI denied women equal protection and that the development of VWIL failed to satisfy the requirement for equal protection, thus agreeing with the court of appeals in its first decision but disagreeing with the court in its decision that Virginia's remedy satisfied that requirement.

Founded in 1839, VMI [Virginia Military Institute] is today the sole single sex school among Virginia's 15 public institutions of higher learning. VMI's distinctive mission is to produce "citizen soldiers," men prepared for leadership in civilian life and in military service. VMI pursues this mission through pervasive training of a kind not available anywhere else in Virginia. Assigning prime place to character development, VMI uses an "adversative method" modeled on English public schools and once characteristic of military instruction. VMI constantly endeavors to instill physical and mental discipline in its cadets and impart to them a strong moral code. The school's graduates leave VMI with heightened comprehension of their capacity to deal with duress and stress, and a large sense of accomplishment for completing the hazardous course.

VMI has notably succeeded in its mission to produce leaders; among its alumni are military generals, Members of Congress, and business executives. The school's alumni overwhelmingly perceive that their VMI training helped them to realize their personal goals. VMI's endowment reflects the loyalty of its graduates; VMI has the largest per student endowment of all undergraduate institutions in the Nation.

Neither the goal of producing citizen soldiers nor VMI's implementing methodology is inherently unsuitable to women. And the school's impressive record in producing leaders has made admission desirable to some women. Nevertheless, Virginia has elected to preserve exclusively for men the advantages and opportunities a VMI education affords. . . .

Issues Raised

In 1990, prompted by a complaint filed with the Attorney General by a female high school student seeking admission to

VMI, the United States sued the Commonwealth of Virginia and VMI, alleging that VMI's exclusively male admission policy violated the Equal Protection Clause of the Fourteenth Amendment. . . .

The cross petitions in this case present two ultimate issues. First, does Virginia's exclusion of women from the educational opportunities provided by VMI—extraordinary opportunities for military training and civilian leadership development—deny to women "capable of all of the individual activities required of VMI cadets," the equal protection of the laws guaranteed by the Fourteenth Amendment? Second, if VMI's "unique" situation—as Virginia's sole single sex public institution of higher education—offends the Constitution's equal protection principle, what is the remedial requirement?

We note, once again, the core instruction of this Court's pathmarking decisions in *J.E.B. v. Alabama ex rel. T.B.* (1994), and *Mississippi Univ. for Women* [*v. Hogan* (1982)]: Parties who seek to defend gender based government action must demonstrate an "exceedingly persuasive justification" for that action. . . .

The Use of Sex Classifications

The heightened review standard our precedent establishes does not make sex a proscribed classification. Supposed "inherent differences" are no longer accepted as a ground for race or national origin classifications. Physical differences between men and women, however, are enduring: "[T]he two sexes are not fungible [interchangeable]; a community made up exclusively of one [sex] is different from a community composed of both" [*Ballard v. United States* (1946)].

"Inherent differences" between men and women, we have come to appreciate, remain cause for celebration, but not for denigration of the members of either sex or for artificial constraints on an individual's opportunity. Sex classifications may be used to compensate women "for particular economic disabilities [they have] suffered" [*Califano v. Webster* (1977)], to "promot[e] equal employment opportunity" [*California Federal Sav. & Loan Assn. v. Guerra* (1987)], to advance full development of the talent and capacities of our Nation's people. But such classifications may not be used, as they once were, to create or perpetuate the legal, social, and economic inferiority of women.

Measuring the record in this case against the review standard just described, we conclude that Virginia has shown no "exceedingly persuasive justification" for excluding all women from the citizen soldier training afforded by VMI. We therefore affirm the Fourth Circuit's initial judgment, which held that Virginia had violated the Fourteenth Amendment's Equal Protection Clause. Because the remedy proffered by Virginia— the Mary Baldwin VWIL [Virginia Women's Institute for Leadership] program—does not cure the constitutional violation, *i.e.* [that is], it does not provide equal opportunity, we reverse the Fourth Circuit's final judgment in this case.

The Value of Single-Sex Education

The Fourth Circuit initially held that Virginia had advanced no state policy by which it could justify, under equal protection principles, its determination "to afford VMI's unique type of program to men and not to women." Virginia challenges that "liability" ruling and asserts two justifications in defense of VMI's exclusion of women. First, the Commonwealth contends, "single sex education provides important educational benefits," and the option of single sex education contributes to "diversity in educational approaches." Second, the Commonwealth argues, "the unique VMI method of character development and leadership training," the school's adversative approach, would have to be modified were VMI to admit women. We consider these two justifications in turn.

Single sex education affords pedagogical benefits to at least some students, Virginia emphasizes, and that reality is uncontested in this litigation. Similarly, it is not disputed that diversity among public educational institutions can serve the public good. But Virginia has not shown that VMI was established, or has been maintained, with a view to diversifying, by its categorical exclusion of women, educational opportunities within the State. In cases of this genre, our precedent instructs that "benign" justifications proffered in defense of categorical exclusions will not be accepted automatically; a tenable justification must describe actual state purposes, not rationalizations for actions in fact differently grounded.

Mississippi Univ. for Women is immediately in point. There the State asserted, in justification of its exclusion of men from a nursing school, that it was engaging in "educational affirmative action" by "compensat[ing] for discrimination against women." Undertaking a "searching analysis," the Court found no close resemblance between "the alleged objective" and "the actual purpose underlying the discriminatory classification." Pursuing a similar inquiry here, we reach the same conclusion. . . .

Furthering Diversity

Our 1982 decision in *Mississippi Univ. for Women* prompted VMI to reexamine its male only admission policy. Virginia relies on that reexamination as a legitimate basis for maintaining VMI's single sex character. A Mission Study Committee, appointed by the VMI Board of Visitors, studied the problem from October 1983 until May 1986, and in that month counseled against "change of VMI status as a single sex college." Whatever internal purpose the Mission Study Committee served—and however well meaning the framers of the report—we can hardly extract from that effort any state policy evenhandedly to advance diverse educational options. As the District Court observed, the Committee's analysis "primarily focuse[d] on anticipated difficulties in attracting females to VMI," and the report, overall, supplied "very little indication of how th[e] conclusion was reached."

In sum, we find no persuasive evidence in this record that VMI's male only admission policy "is in furtherance of a state policy of 'diversity.'" No such policy, the Fourth Circuit observed, can be discerned from the movement of all other public colleges and universities in Virginia away from single sex education. That court also questioned "how one institution with autonomy, but with no authority over any other state institution, can give effect to a state policy of diversity among institutions." A purpose genuinely to advance an array of educational options, as the Court of Appeals recognized, is not served by VMI's historic and constant plan—a plan to "affor[d] a unique educational benefit only to males." However "liberally" this plan serves the State's sons, it makes no provision whatever for her daughters. That is not *equal* protection.

The Accommodation of Women

Virginia next argues that VMI's adversative method of training provides educational benefits that cannot be made available, unmodified, to women. Alterations to accommodate women would necessarily be "radical," so "drastic," Virginia asserts, as to transform, indeed "destroy," VMI's program. Neither sex would be favored by the transformation, Virginia maintains: Men would be deprived of the unique opportunity currently available to them; women would not gain that opportunity because their participation would "eliminat[e] the very aspects of [the] program that distinguish [VMI] from . . . other institutions of higher education in Virginia."

The District Court forecast from expert witness testimony, and the Court of Appeals accepted, that coeducation would materially affect "at least these three aspects of VMI's program—physical training, the absence of privacy, and the adversative approach." And it is uncontested that women's admission would require accommodations, primarily in arranging housing assignments and physical training programs for female cadets. It is also undisputed, however, that "the VMI methodology could be used to educate women." The District Court even allowed that some women may prefer it to the methodology a women's college might pursue. "[S]ome women, at least, would want to attend [VMI] if they had the opportunity," the District Court recognized, and "some women," the expert testimony established, "are capable of all of the individual activities required of VMI cadets." The parties, furthermore, agree that "*some* women can meet the physical standards [VMI] now impose[s] on men." In sum, as the Court of Appeals stated, "neither the goal of producing citizen soldiers," VMI's *raison d'être* [reason for being], "nor VMI's implementing methodology is inherently unsuitable to women." . . .

Women's successful entry into the federal military academies, and their participation in the Nation's military forces, indicate that Virginia's fears for the future of VMI may not be solidly grounded. The State's justification for excluding all women from "citizen soldier" training for which some are qualified, in any event, cannot rank as "exceedingly persuasive," as we have explained and applied that standard. . . .

The State's misunderstanding and, in turn, the District Court's, is apparent from VMI's mission: to produce "citizen soldiers," individuals

> "imbued with love of learning, confident in the functions and attitudes of leadership, possessing a high sense of public service, advocates of the American democracy and free enterprise system, and ready . . . to defend their country in time of national peril."

Surely that goal is great enough to accommodate women, who today count as citizens in our American democracy equal in stature to men. Just as surely, the State's great goal is not substantially advanced by women's categorical exclusion, in total disregard of their individual merit, from the State's premier "citizen soldier" corps. Virginia, in sum, "has fallen far short of establishing the 'exceedingly persuasive justification'" [*Mississippi Univ. for Women*], that must be the solid base for any gender defined classification.

Virginia's Remedial Plan

In the second phase of the litigation, Virginia presented its remedial plan—maintain VMI as a male only college and create VWIL as a separate program for women. The plan met District Court approval. The Fourth Circuit, in turn, deferentially reviewed the State's proposal and decided that the two single sex programs directly served Virginia's reasserted purposes: single gender education, and "achieving the results of an adversative method in a military environment." Inspecting the VMI and VWIL educational programs to determine whether they "afford[ed] to both genders benefits comparable in substance, [if] not in form and detail," the Court of Appeals concluded that Virginia had arranged for men and women opportunities "sufficiently comparable" to survive equal protection evaluation. The United States challenges this "remedial" ruling as pervasively misguided.

A remedial decree, this Court has said, must closely fit the constitutional violation; it must be shaped to place persons unconstitutionally denied an opportunity or advantage in "the position they would have occupied in the absence of [discrimination]." The constitutional violation in this case is the categorical exclusion of women from an extraordinary educational opportunity afforded men. A proper remedy for an unconstitutional exclusion, we have explained, aims to "eliminate [so far as possible] the discriminatory effects of the past" and to "bar like discrimination in the future." [*Louisiana v. United States* (1965)]

Virginia chose not to eliminate, but to leave untouched, VMI's exclusionary policy. For women only, however, Virginia proposed a separate program, different in kind from VMI and unequal in tangible and intangible facilities. Having violated the Constitution's equal protection requirement, Virginia was obliged to show that its remedial proposal "directly address[ed] and relate[d] to" the violation [*Milliken v. Bradley* (1977)], the equal protection dented to women ready, willing, and able to benefit from educational opportunities of the kind VMI offers. Virginia described VWIL as a "parallel program," and asserted that VWIL shares VMI's mission of producing "citizen soldiers" and VMI's goals of providing "education, military training, mental and physical discipline, character . . . and leadership development." If the VWIL program could not "eliminate the discriminatory effects of the past," could it at least "bar like discrimination in the future"? A comparison of the programs said to be "parallel" informs our answer. In exposing the character of, and differences in, the VMI and VWIL programs, we recapitulate facts earlier presented.

Differences Between VMI and VWIL

VWIL affords women no opportunity to experience the rigorous military training for which VMI is famed. Instead, the VWIL program "deemphasize[s]" military education, and uses a "cooperative method" of education "which reinforces self esteem."

VWIL students participate in ROTC [Reserve Officers Training Corps] and a "largely ceremonial" Virginia Corps of Cadets, but Virginia deliberately did not make VWIL a military institute. The VWIL House is not a military style residence and VWIL students need not live together throughout the 4 year program, eat meals together, or wear uniforms during the school day. VWIL students thus do not experience the "barracks" life "crucial to the VMI experience," the spartan living arrangements designed to foster an "egalitarian ethic." "[T]he most important aspects of the VMI educational experience occur in the barracks," the District Court found, yet Virginia deemed that core experience nonessential, indeed inappropriate, for training its female citizen soldiers.

VWIL students receive their "leadership training" in seminars, externships, and speaker series, episodes and encounters lacking the "[p]hysical rigor, mental stress, . . . minute regulation of behavior, and indoctrination in desirable values" made hallmarks of VMI's citizen soldier training. Kept away from the pressures, hazards, and psychological bonding characteristic of VMI's adversative training, VWIL students will not know the "feeling of tremendous accomplishment" commonly experienced by VMI's successful cadets.

Virginia maintains that these methodological differences are "justified pedagogically," based on "important differences between men and women in learning and developmental needs," "psychological and sociological differences" Virginia describes as "real" and "not stereotypes." The Task Force charged with developing the leadership program for women, drawn from the staff and faculty at Mary Baldwin College, "determined that a military model and, especially VMI's adversative method, would be wholly inappropriate for educating and training most women." The Commonwealth embraced the Task Force view, as did expert witnesses who testified for Virginia.

As earlier stated, generalizations about "the way women are," estimates of what is appropriate for *most women*, no longer justify denying opportunity to women whose talent and capacity place them outside the average description. Notably, Virginia never asserted that VMI's method of education suits *most men*. It is also revealing that Virginia accounted for its failure to make the VWIL experience "the entirely militaristic experience of VMI" on the ground that VWIL "is planned for women who do not necessarily expect to pursue military careers." By that reasoning, VMI's "entirely militaristic" program would be inappropriate for men in general or *as a group*, for "[o]nly about 15% of VMI cadets enter career military service."

In contrast to the generalizations about women on which Virginia rests, we note again these dispositive realties: VMI's "implementing methodology" is not "inherently unsuitable to women," "some women . . . do well under [the] adversative model," "some women, at least, would want to attend [VMI] if they had the opportunity," "some women are capable of all of the individual activities required of VMI cadets," and "can meet the physical standards [VMI] now impose[s] on men." It is on behalf of these women that the United States has instituted this suit, and it is for them that a remedy must be crafted, a remedy that will end their exclusion from a state supplied educational opportunity for which they are fit, a decree that will "bar like discrimination in the future."

In myriad respects other than military training, VWIL does not qualify as VMI's equal. VWIL's student body, faculty, course offerings, and facilities hardly match VMI's. Nor can the VWIL graduate anticipate the benefits associated with VMI's 157-year history, the school's prestige, and its influential alumni network. . . .

Genuine Equal Protection for Women

Virginia, in sum, while maintaining VMI for men only, has failed to provide any "comparable single gender women's institution." Instead, the Commonwealth has created a VWIL program fairly appraised as a "pale shadow" of VMI in terms of the range of curricular choices and faculty stature, funding, prestige, alumni support and influence. . . .

VMI, too, offers an educational opportunity no other Virginia institution provides, and the school's "prestige"—associated with its success in developing "citizen soldiers"—is unequaled. Virginia has closed this facility to its daughters and, instead, has devised for them a "parallel program," with a faculty less impressively credentialed and less well paid, more limited course offerings, fewer opportunities for military training and for scientific specialization. VMI, beyond question, "possesses to a far greater degree" than the VWIL program "those qualities which are incapable of objective measurement but which make for greatness in a . . . school," including "position and influence of the alumni, standing in the community, traditions and prestige" [*Sweatt v. Painter* (1950)]. Women seeking and fit for a VMI quality education cannot be offered anything less, under the State's obligation to afford them genuinely equal protection.

A prime part of the history of our Constitution, historian Richard Morris recounted, is the story of the extension of constitutional rights and protections to people once ignored or excluded. VMI's story continued as our comprehension of "We the People" expanded. There is no reason to believe that the admission of women capable of all the activities required of VMI cadets would destroy the Institute rather than enhance its capacity to serve the "more perfect Union."

"The enemies of single sex education have won; by persuading only seven Justices . . . that their view of the world is enshrined in the Constitution."

Dissenting Opinion: Single-Sex Schools Are Not Unconstitutional

Antonin Scalia

Antonin Scalia has been a member of the U.S. Supreme Court since 1986, when he was appointed by President Ronald Reagan. He is known for his conservatism, particularly his commitment to the doctrine of originalism, or adhering to the original intent of the Framers in interpreting the U.S. Constitution.

The following excerpt is from Scalia's dissent in United States v. Virginia. *He disagrees with the Court's decision, which determined that the Virginia Military Institute's (VMI) male-only admission policy violated the equal protection clause of the Fourteenth Amendment. Scalia claims that there is nothing in the Constitution to prevent a state from deciding to have a single-sex school as long as they have a reason for doing so that is related to an important state objective. Scalia claims that the Court subjected the state's justification for the single-sex policy to far too much scrutiny. He believes that expanding VMI admission to women is an issue for the state legislature to decide and not a policy that the Court has power to override based on anything in the U.S. Constitution.*

Antonin Scalia, dissenting opinion, *United States v. Virginia*, U.S. Supreme Court, June 26, 1996.

Much of the Court's opinion is devoted to deprecating the closed mindedness of our forebears with regard to women's education, and even with regard to the treatment of women in areas that have nothing to do with education. Closed minded they were—as every age is, including our own, with regard to matters it cannot guess, because it simply does not consider them debatable. The virtue of a democratic system with a First Amendment is that it readily enables the people, over time, to be persuaded that what they took for granted is not so, and to change their laws accordingly. That system is destroyed if the smug assurances of each age are removed from the democratic process and written into the Constitution. So to counterbalance the Court's criticism of our ancestors, let me say a word in their praise: they left us free to change. The same cannot be said of this most illiberal Court, which has embarked on a course of inscribing one after another of the current preferences of the society (and in some cases only the counter majoritarian preferences of the society's law trained elite) into our Basic Law. Today it enshrines the notion that no substantial educational value is to be served by an all men's military academy—so that the decision by the people of Virginia to maintain such an institution denies equal protection to women who cannot attend that institution but can attend others. Since it is entirely clear that the Constitution of the United States—the old one—takes no sides in this educational debate, I dissent. . . .

The Importance of Tradition

I have no problem with a system of abstract tests such as rational basis, intermediate, and strict scrutiny (though I think we can do better than applying strict scrutiny and intermediate scrutiny whenever we feel like it). Such formulas are essential to evaluating whether the new restrictions that a changing society constantly imposes upon private conduct comport with that "equal protection" our society has always accorded in the past. But in my view the function of this Court is to *preserve* our society's values regarding (among other things) equal protection, not to *revise* them; to prevent backsliding from the degree of restriction the Constitution imposed upon democratic government, not to prescribe, on our own authority, progressively higher degrees. For that reason it is my view that, whatever abstract tests we may choose to devise, they cannot supersede—and indeed ought to be crafted *so as to reflect*—those constant and unbroken national traditions that embody the people's understanding of ambiguous constitutional texts. More specifically, it is my view that "when a practice not expressly prohibited by the text of the Bill of Rights bears the endorsement of a long tradition of open, widespread, and unchallenged use that dates back to the beginning of the Republic, we have no proper basis for striking it down" [*Rutan v. Republican Party of Ill.* (1990) (Scalia, J., dissenting)]. The same applies, *mutatis mutandis* [with the necessary changes made] to a practice asserted to be in violation of the post–Civil War Fourteenth Amendment.

The all male constitution of VMI [Virginia Military Institute] comes squarely within such a governing tradition. Founded by the Commonwealth of Virginia in 1839 and continuously maintained by it since, VMI has always admitted only men. And in that regard it has not been unusual. For almost all of VMI's more than a century and a half of existence, its single sex status reflected the uniform practice for government supported military colleges. Another famous Southern institution, The Citadel, has existed as a state funded school of South Carolina since 1842. And all the federal military colleges—West Point, the Naval Academy at Annapolis, and even the Air Force Academy, which was not established until 1954—admitted only males for most of their history. Their admission of women in 1976 (upon which the Court today relies), came not by court decree, but because the people, through their elected representatives, decreed a change. In other words, the tradition of having government funded military schools for men is as well rooted in the traditions of this country as the tradition of sending only men into military combat. The people may decide to change the one tradition, like the other, through democratic processes; but the assertion that either tradition has been unconstitutional through the centuries is not law, but politics smuggled into law.

And the same applies, more broadly, to single sex education in general, which, as I shall discuss, is threatened by today's decision with the cut off of all state and federal support. Government run *non*military educational institutions for the two sexes have until very recently also been part of our national tradition. "[It is] [c]oeducation, historically, [that] is a novel educational theory. From grade school through high school, college, and graduate and professional training, much of the Nation's population during much of our history has been educated in sexually segregated classrooms" [*Mississippi Univ. for Women v. Hogan* (1982) (Powell, J., dissenting)]. These traditions may of course be changed by the democratic decisions of the people, as they largely have been.

The Correct Test

Today, however, change is forced upon Virginia, and reversion to single sex education is prohibited nationwide, not by democratic processes but by order of this Court. Even while bemoaning the sorry, bygone days of "fixed notions" concerning women's education, the Court favors current notions so fixedly that it is willing to write them into the Constitution of the United States by application of custom built "tests." This is not the interpretation of a Constitution, but the creation of one.

To reject the Court's disposition today, however, it is not necessary to accept my view that the Court's made up tests cannot displace longstanding national traditions as the primary determinant of what the Constitution means. It is only necessary to apply honestly the test the Court has been applying to sex based classifications for the past two decades. It is well settled, as Justice [Sandra Day] O'Connor stated some time ago for a unanimous Court, that we evaluate a statutory classification based on sex under a standard that lies "[b]etween th[e] extremes of rational basis review and strict scrutiny" [*Clark v. Jeter* (1988)]. We have denominated this standard "intermediate scrutiny" and under it have inquired whether the statutory classification is "substantially related to an important governmental objective." . . .

Only the amorphous "exceedingly persuasive justification" phrase, and not the standard elaboration of intermediate scrutiny, can be made to yield this conclusion that VMI's single sex composition is unconstitutional because there exist several women (or, one would have to conclude under the Court's reasoning, a single woman) willing and able to undertake VMI's program. Intermediate scrutiny has never required a least restrictive means analysis, but only a "substantial relation" between the classification and the state interests that it serves. Thus, in *Califano v. Webster* (1977), we upheld a congressional statute that provided higher Social Security benefits for women than for men. We reasoned that "women . . . as such have been unfairly hindered from earning as much as men," but we did not require proof that each woman so benefited had suffered discrimination or that each disadvantaged man had not; it was sufficient that even under the former congressional scheme "women *on the average* received lower retirement benefits than men" (emphasis added). The reasoning in our other intermediate scrutiny cases has similarly required only a substantial relation between end and means, not a perfect fit. In *Rostker v. Goldberg* (1981), we held that selective service registration could constitutionally exclude women, because even "assuming that a small number of women could be drafted for noncombat roles, Congress simply did not consider it worth the added burdens of including women in draft and registration plans." . . . There is simply no support in our cases for the notion that a sex based classification is invalid unless it relates to characteristics that hold true in every instance. . . .

Virginia's Interest in Single-Sex Education

With this explanation of how the Court has succeeded in making its analysis seem orthodox—and indeed, if intimations are to be believed, even overly generous to VMI—I now proceed to describe how the analysis should have been conducted. The question to be answered, I repeat, is whether the exclusion of women from VMI is "substantially related to an important governmental objective."

It is beyond question that Virginia has an important state interest in providing effective college education for its citizens. That single sex instruction is an approach substantially related to that interest should be evident enough from the long and continuing history in this country of men's and women's colleges. But beyond that, as the Court of Appeals here stated: "That single gender education at the college level is beneficial to both sexes is a *fact established in this case*" (emphasis added).

The evidence establishing that fact was overwhelming—indeed, "virtually uncontradicted" in the words of the court that received the evidence. As an initial matter, Virginia demonstrated at trial that "[a] substantial body of contemporary scholarship and research supports the proposition that, although males and females have significant areas of developmental overlap, they also have differing developmental needs that are deep seated." While no one questioned that for many students a coeducational environment was nonetheless not inappropriate, that could not obscure the demonstrated benefits of single sex colleges. For example, the District Court stated as follows:

"One empirical study in evidence, not questioned by any expert, demonstrates that single sex colleges provide better educational experiences than coeducational institutions. Students of both sexes become more academically involved, interact with faculty frequently, show larger increases in intellectual self esteem and are more satisfied with practically all aspects of college experience (the sole exception is social life) compared with their counterparts in coeducational institutions. Attendance at an all male college substantially increases the likelihood that a student will carry out career plans in law, business and college teaching, and also has a substantial positive effect on starting salaries in business. Women's colleges increase the chances that those who attend will obtain positions of leadership, complete the baccalaureate degree, and aspire to higher degrees."

"[I]n the light of this very substantial authority favoring single sex education," the District Court concluded that "the VMI Board's decision to maintain an all male institution is fully justified even without taking into consideration the other unique features of VMI's teaching and training." This finding alone, which even this Court cannot dispute, should be sufficient to demonstrate the constitutionality of VMI's all male composition.

A Distinctive Educational Method

But besides its single sex constitution, VMI is different from other colleges in another way. It employs a "distinctive educational method," sometimes referred to as the "adversative, or doubting, model of education." "Physical rigor, mental stress, absolute equality of treatment, absence of privacy, minute regulation of behavior, and indoctrination in desirable values are the salient attributes of the VMI educational experience." No one contends that this method is appropriate for all individuals; education is not a "one size fits all" business. Just as a State may wish to support junior colleges, vocational institutes, or a law school that emphasizes case practice instead of classroom study, so too a State's decision to maintain within its system one school that provides the adversative method is "substantially related" to its goal of good education. Moreover, it was uncontested that "if the state were to establish a women's VMI type [*i.e.*, adversative] program, the program would attract an insufficient number of participants to make the program work," and it was found by the District Court that if Virginia were to include women in VMI, the school "would eventually find it necessary to drop the adversative system altogether." Thus, Virginia's options were an adversative method that excludes women or no adversative method at all.

There can be no serious dispute that, as the District Court found, single sex education and a distinctive educational method "represent legitimate contributions to diversity in the Virginia higher education system." As a theoretical matter, Virginia's educational interest would have been *best* served (insofar as the two factors we have mentioned are concerned) by six different types of public colleges—an all men's, an all women's, and a coeducational college run in the "adversative method," and an all men's, an all women's, and a coeducational college run in the "traditional method." But as a practical matter, of course, Virginia's financial resources, like any State's, are not limitless, and the Commonwealth must select among the available options. Virginia thus has decided to fund, in addition to some 14 coeducational 4 year colleges, one college that is run as an all male school on the adversative model: the Virginia Military Institute.

Virginia did not make this determination regarding the make up of its public college system on the unrealistic assumption that no other colleges exist. Substantial evidence in the District Court demonstrated that the Commonwealth has long proceeded on the principle that "[h]igher education resources should be viewed as a whole—public and private—" because such an approach enhances diversity and because "it is academic and economic waste to permit unwarranted duplication." It is thus significant that, whereas there are "four all female private [colleges] in Virginia," there is only "one private all male college," which "indicates that the private sector is providing for th[e] [former] form of education to a much greater extent that it provides for all male education." In these circumstances, Virginia's election to fund one public all male institution and one on the adversative model—and to concentrate its resources in a single entity that serves both these interests in diversity—is substantially related to the State's important educational interests. . . .

The Function of the Court

As is frequently true, the Court's decision today will have consequences that extend far beyond the parties to the case. What I take to be the Court's unease with these consequences, and its resulting unwillingness to acknowledge them, cannot alter the reality.

Under the constitutional principles announced and applied today, single sex public education is unconstitutional. By going through the motions of applying a balancing test—asking whether the State has adduced an "exceedingly persuasive justification" for its sex based classification—the Court creates the illusion that government officials in some future case will have a clear shot at justifying some sort of single sex public education. Indeed, the Court seeks to create even a greater illusion than that: It purports to have said nothing of relevance to *other* public schools at all. "We address specifically and only an educational opportunity recognized . . . as unique. . . ."

The Supreme Court of the United States does not sit to announce "unique" dispositions. Its principal function is to establish *precedent*—that is, to set forth principles of law that every court in America must follow. As we said only this Term, we expect both ourselves and lower courts to adhere to the "*rationale* upon which the Court based the results of its earlier decisions" [*Seminole Tribe of Fla. v. Florida* (1996)] (emphasis added). That is the principal reason we publish our opinions.

And the rationale of today's decision is sweeping: for sex based classifications, a redefinition of intermediate scrutiny that makes it indistinguishable from strict scrutiny. Indeed, the Court indicates that if any program restricted to one sex is "uniqu[e]," it must be opened to members of the opposite sex "who have the will and capacity" to participate in it. I suggest that the single sex program that will not be capable of being characterized as "unique" is not only unique but nonexistent.

End of Single-Sex Public Education

In any event, regardless of whether the Court's rationale leaves some small amount of room for lawyers to argue, it ensures that single sex public education is functionally dead. The costs of litigating the constitutionality of a single sex education program, and the risks of ultimately losing that litigation, are simply too high to be embraced by public officials. Any person with standing to challenge any sex based classification can haul the State into federal court and compel it to establish by evidence (presumably in the form of expert testimony) that there is an "exceedingly persuasive justification" for the classification. Should the courts happen to interpret that vacuous phrase as establishing a standard that is not utterly impossible of achievement, there is considerable risk that whether the standard has been met will not be determined on the basis of the record evidence—indeed, that will necessarily be the approach of any court that seeks to walk the path the Court has trod today. No state official in his right mind will buy such a high cost, high risk lawsuit by commencing a single sex program. The enemies of single sex education have won; by persuading only seven Justices (five would have been enough) that their view of the world is enshrined in the Constitution, they have effectively imposed that view on all 50 States.

This is especially regrettable because, as the District Court here determined, educational experts in recent years have increasingly come to "suppor[t] [the] view that substantial educational benefits flow from a single gender environment, be it male or female, *that cannot be replicated in a coeducational setting*" (emphasis added). "The evidence in th[is] case," for example, "is virtually uncontradicted" to that effect. Until quite recently, some public officials have attempted to institute new single sex programs, at least as experiments. In 1991, for example, the Detroit Board of Education announced a program to establish three boys only schools for inner city youth; it was met with a lawsuit, a preliminary injunction was swiftly entered by a District Court that purported to rely on *Hogan*, and the Detroit Board of Education voted to abandon the litigation and thus abandon the plan. Today's opinion assures that no such experiment will be tried again.

There are few extant single sex public educational programs. The potential of today's decision for widespread disruption of existing institutions lies in its application to *private* single sex education. Government support is immensely important to private educational institutions. . . .

The only hope for state assisted single sex private schools is that the Court will not apply in the future the principles of law it has applied today. That is a substantial hope, I am happy and ashamed to say. After all, did not the Court today abandon the principles of law it has applied in our earlier sex classification cases? And does not the Court positively invite private colleges to rely upon our ad hocery by assuring them this case is "unique"? I would not advise the foundation of any new single sex college (especially an all male one) with the expectation of being allowed to receive any government support; but it is too soon to abandon in despair those single sex colleges already in existence. It will certainly be possible for this Court to write a future opinion that ignores the broad principles of law set forth today, and that characterizes as utterly dispositive the opinion's perceptions that VMI was a uniquely prestigious all male institution, conceived in chauvinism, etc., etc. I will not join that opinion.

"Rather than narrowing the range of educational options available to women . . . the VMI decision supports an expansive view of equal educational opportunity for both sexes."

United States v. Virginia Is a Victory for Equal Opportunity for Women

Rosemary C. Salomone

Rosemary C. Salomone is the Kenneth Wang Professor of Law at St. John's University in New York. She is the author of Same, Different, Equal: Rethinking Single-Sex Schooling.

In the following article, Salomone celebrates the Supreme Court decision in United States v. Virginia, *wherein the Court found the male-only admission policy of the Virginia Military Institute unconstitutional. Salomone claims that the decision advanced gender equality by rejecting traditional gender classifications as justification for single-sex education. Although critics have worried that the decision will eliminate all single-sex schooling, Salomone claims that such a worry is unfounded, concluding that single-sex institutions that exist to challenge traditional gender classifications rather than uphold them are consistent with the Court's decision. Salomone concludes that it is not clear whether the Court's strengthened review of the gender classification in* Virginia *will have a lasting effect on how the Court views gender cases, improving gender equality as she believes it has in this case.*

Rosemary C. Salomone, "The VMI Case: Affirmation of Equal Opportunity for Women," Trial, vol. 32, October 1996, pp. 67–70. Copyright © 1996 American Association for Justice, formerly Association of Trial Lawyers of America (ATLA). Reproduced by permission.

The recent Supreme Court decision striking down the exclusion of women from the Virginia Military Institute (VMI), a state-supported institution of higher education, represents a victory for the principle of equal opportunity for girls and women at all levels of education.

While the Court's decision is narrow in scope, addressing the particular circumstances of an almost unique single-sex military institution, the depth and breadth of the majority's logic make the VMI case one of the high-water marks in the 20th-century struggle to overcome stereotypes of women and to validate women's constitutional right to be treated with respect equal to men.

The Complaint About VMI

Established in 1839, VMI remains the only single-sex institution within the Virginia state system. All other public colleges and universities became coeducational by the mid-1970s. While VMI's educational approach is grounded in a physically and psychologically demanding program typical of military training, the institution's primary objective of producing citizen-soldiers is far broader.

Only 15 percent of its graduates enter career military service, with many of the remainder moving on to leadership positions in business and public life.

The tortuous litigation leading up to this [the 1996] Supreme Court decision began in 1990 when a complaint filed with the state attorney general by a female high school student seeking admission to VMI prompted the United States to sue the state of Virginia and the institute. The Justice Department maintained that VMI's all-male admissions policy violated the Equal Protection Clause of the Fourteenth Amendment. The district court ruled in favor of VMI.

The Fourth Circuit Court of Appeals vacated the ruling and remanded the case, finding the school's policy unconstitutional. The appeals court suggested that Virginia might consider changing the program so as to admit women, establishing a parallel publicly supported institution or program for women, or completely abandoning state support.

The state subsequently proposed a separate program, the Virginia Women's Institute for Leadership, to be supported with state funds at Mary Baldwin College, a private liberal arts school for women. The district court upheld and ordered implementation of the plan. A divided appeals court affirmed, finding that the two programs were "substantively comparable."

Following the Fourth Circuit's denial of a rehearing en banc [by the full court] the Supreme Court granted the United States's petition for certiorari [a request to review a lower court's finding], setting the stage for the Court to make its first major statement on gender equality in more than a decade.

The Court's Opinion

In an artfully yet forcefully crafted majority opinion joined five other justices, with Chief Justice William Rehnquist concurring in conclusion, Justice Ruth Bader Ginsburg drew on three decades of Court precedent, citing many cases she herself had argued before the Court on behalf of gender equality. The opinion clarifies lingering confusion over the legal and social parameters of women's place in society and the complex role that educational access plays in supporting the constitutional value of equality.

The majority's sweeping rationale, however, lends itself to possible misinterpretation and distortion. It also provokes a reactionary response in some people grounded in traditional views of male and female roles, as clearly evidenced in Justice Antonin Scalia's lone dissent.

Undoubtedly mindful yet undaunted by the inevitable counterattack, a solid majority on the Court seized the opportunity to forge new ground on Fourteenth Amendment equal protection for women. In so doing, the Court struck a blow at archaic notions of women's capabilities and tendencies, while reaffirming the permissibility of gender categorizations under certain circumstances, including state-supported single-sex educational programs and institutions.

From a legal perspective, the majority placed a new spin on two decades of Fourteenth Amendment equal protection analysis. The majority did not merely reaffirm a standard of judicial review applied to gender classifications in prior cases, where the program or policy must be "substantially" related to an "important" government interest.

Instead, the language moved gender equality one small but significant step closer on the Court's analytic continuum toward the more exacting judicial standard applied to racial classifications. Here the state policy must represent the "least restrictive means" for promoting a "compelling" government interest to pass constitutional muster. These ambiguous "words of art" have engaged the courts in endless intellectual gymnastics and borne significantly divergent results in myriad decisions over the years.

Although not moving completely to a "compelling interest" test, the majority nevertheless restated and applied with a "bite" the standard used in gender discrimination cases for the past two decades.

The State's Justifications

The majority noted that courts must apply "skeptical scrutiny," taking a "hard look" at "generalizations or tendencies" based on gender. It further noted that the state of Virginia must advance not just a "substantial" but an "exceedingly persuasive justification" for categorically excluding women from the Virginia Military Institute.

The majority viewed this latter standard as the "core instruction" of the Court's prior decisions on gender. In fact, the majority's emphasis on the fact that at least some women are capable of succeeding under VMI's demanding program suggests a closer fit between means and ends than required in prior cases.

The state advanced two justifications for excluding women from VMI: to provide diversity to an otherwise coeducational state system of higher education and to preserve VMI's unique "adversative" approach. State officials argued this approach, featuring constant surveillance, the absence of privacy, a hierarchical system of class privileges and responsibilities, and a stringently enforced honor code, was inherently unsuitable for women and would be materially compromised by coeducation.

The Court found neither justification to be "exceedingly persuasive," rejecting in particular lower court findings on gender-based developmental differences that pointed to typically male and female "tendencies." As for the state's argument supporting diversity, the Court concluded that VMI's "historic and constant" plan to provide this unique educational benefit only to men served only the "state's sons," while making "no provision whatever for her daughters."

Gender and Race

Evaluating the state's proposed separate leadership program, the majority opinion drew on race precedent, particularly the Court's 1977 decision in *Milliken v. Bradley*, a school desegregation case. In so doing, the Court imposed what has come to be known as the "tailoring principle," where the remedy must "closely fit" the constitutional violation.

The majority concluded that the separate leadership program did not meet this standard, having failed to "cure" the violation. Drawing on the rationale of *Sweatt v. Painter* [1950], a seminal case in the desegregation of higher education, the Court noted that equality must be measured by both tangibles and intangibles and concluded that the alternative program for women was but "a pale shadow of VMI" in terms of curricular and extracurricular choices, faculty stature, funding, prestige, library resources, and alumni support and influence.

These were the same indices used by the NAACP [National Association for the Advancement of Colored People] in a series of higher education cases dating from the 1930s, leading up to *Sweatt* and culminating in *Brown v. Board of Education* [1954]. The VMI case, in fact, realized *Brown's* promise of equality for women more fully than any prior Court decision on gender.

Nevertheless, the majority in the VMI case did not go so far as to espouse *Brown's* fundamental holding that "separate is inherently unequal" and is unconstitutional in all cases. Nor did the justices deny "inherent differences" between men and women, which the Court tells us "remain cause for celebration, but not for denigration of the members of either sex or for artificial constraints on an individual's opportunity."

As long as there are some women who have the will and capabilities to function successfully under the physically and psychologically rigorous "adversative" method, the state cannot deny them the training and opportunities that VMI uniquely affords.

Single-Sex Education

It is on this score that Ginsburg and her colleagues made the most pronounced social and political statements on gender equality, statements that must be clearly understood by society at large and by the legal and educational establishments in particular. Despite Scalia's speculations concerning the dangerous consequences that would flow to single-sex institutions from this case, the majority made clear that gender classifications may be used in some circumstances to "advance full development of the talent and capacities of our nation's people," but they may not be used to "create or perpetuate the legal, social, and economic inferiority of women."

Implicit in this distinction is a recognition of the now well-documented benefits that women in particular derive from single-sex education, including the opportunity to develop self-esteem and leadership skills that lead to enhanced levels of professional success.

Studies reveal that women who attend these academically challenging colleges are more likely to enter traditionally male-dominated careers such as law, medicine, corporate management, and public office than those who attend coeducational institutions.

Other studies have found similar benefits at the secondary school level. Girls who attend single-sex high schools, as compared to their coeducational counterparts, tend to demonstrate higher educational aspirations, more self-confidence, and less stereotypical views of gender roles. They tend to take more math and science courses at higher levels and achieve higher scores on general academic and science tests.

Research further demonstrates that the gains made by girls in single-sex schools continue even when they choose coed colleges. They not only attend more selective institutions, but they tend to choose nontraditional careers.

With an apparent nod to these types of findings, the Court more directly responded to arguments advanced in a friend-of-the-court brief submitted by 26 private women's colleges, recognizing "the mission of some single-sex schools to 'dissipate, rather than perpetuate, traditional gender classifications.'"

The Court reaffirmed the "state's prerogative evenhandedly to support diverse educational opportunities," contrasting this with the VMI situation, where Virginia denied to women a unique educational opportunity available solely at the state's "premier military institute." Given the history of pervasive exclusionary policies within higher education until recent decades, the Court suggested that the all-male college is very likely to be a device for "preserving tacit assumptions of male superiority."

Primary, Secondary, and Private Schools

It is this aspect of the VMI decision, the continued legality of single-sex institutions, that bears the most immediate impact on education policy. Scalia, in dissent, suggested that this decision could forebode dangerous implications for public single-sex secondary schools, which are now few in number, and particularly for the far more numerous private single-sex schools and colleges.

This "list of horribles"—from loss of tax deductions and loss of tax exemptions as charitable institutions within the private sector to the risk of costly litigation for all—must be swiftly dismissed. If not, it may prod wary educators and policymakers into compliance with legal standards that do not exist.

The recent opposition mounted by the New York Civil Liberties Union, with the ink barely dry on the VMI decision, against a newly established all-girls public secondary school for academic achievers is a clear case in point.

As noted, the majority left open the constitutional door to publicly supported single-sex institutions under certain circumstances. As for the decision's impact on the private sector, the claim brought against VMI was based on the Fourteenth Amendment's Equal Protection Clause, which applies only to state actors. It excludes private institutions from its sweep. It is settled law that government funding and regulation alone, no matter how extensive, cannot turn a private institution into a state actor for purposes of the Fourteenth Amendment.

Furthermore, while the Supreme Court has denied tax benefits to educational institutions that violate national policy against racial discrimination, the majority in this case made no suggestion that similar national policy consensus exists in opposition to private single-sex educational institutions or that there may be a spillover into the enforcement of federal tax laws as a result of the decision.

Most important, Title IX of the Education Amendments of 1972, which prohibits sex discrimination in federally funded programs and activities in both public and private institutions, implicitly excludes from its coverage the admissions policies of elementary and secondary schools (with the exception of vocational schools) as well as private undergraduate institutions.

In other words, given the current status of both constitutional and statutory law at least at the federal level, the legal tools simply do not exist to successfully attack public elementary and secondary or private single-sex schools or colleges (except graduate and vocational programs) in the courts.

And given the majority's implicit recognition of the benefits of single-sex education where choice and diversity are real and not pretextual, it is highly unlikely that this Court will attempt to remove those protections through constitutional interpretation.

A Controversial Case

The VMI case will remain controversial for years to come, evoking as it does in majority and dissent distinctly divergent perspectives on women and on the role of the Court in articulating public values and shaping public policy through the Constitution.

It remains to be seen whether the Court's strengthened standard of review is but a momentary digression or a firmly rooted approach that may significantly influence the course of gender equality. If the latter, then the Court's "hard look," "skeptical scrutiny" review may bear on curricular and extra-curricular offerings, particularly where public schools and colleges provide different athletic opportunities to male and female students based on stereotypical assumptions of women's interests.

What is clear, however, is that the Supreme Court has spoken out persuasively against the categorical exclusion of women based on as ephemeral and outmoded a concept as "traditional" notions of "typical" female and male "tendencies." Rather than narrowing the range of educational options available to women, as political and judicial pundits suggest, the VMI decision supports an expansive view of equal educational opportunity for both sexes, a view that permits educational distinctness and choice so long as the objective and the result are to provide equal access.

"We should all be concerned by the majority's willingness in the V.M.I. case to ignore the evidence in the record, its own precedent, and Congress."

United States v. Virginia Wrongly Ignored Evidence, Precedent, and Congress

William G. Broaddus

William G. Broaddus is the former attorney general of Virginia and a practicing lawyer, involved as co-counsel in representing the Virginia Military Institute and the Commonwealth of Virginia in United States v. Virginia.

In the following article, Broaddus states that the Supreme Court erred in its 1996 decision in United States v. Virginia, *which found the male-only admissions policy of the Virginia Military Institute (VMI) to violate the equal protection clause of the Fourteenth Amendment. Broaddus claims that the Court's own precedent, or past rulings, supported a different outcome. In addition, he says that the Court ignored evidence in the case that supported the continuation of VMI's male-only policy and the effectiveness of the parallel all-women's program created for women interested in an educational experience similar to VMI. Finally, Broaddus argues that the Court overstepped its bounds in the* Virginia *decision, contradicting the express desires of Congress.*

William G. Broaddus, "Is the VMI Decision an Omen or an Aberration?" *Chronicle of Higher Education*, vol. 42, July 12, 1996, p. A48. Copyright © 1996 by The Chronicle of Higher Education. Reproduced by permission of the author.

The Supreme Court's recent decision in *United States v. Virginia*, striking down the all-male admissions policy at the state-supported Virginia Military Institute [V.M.I.], is a lamentable example of the judiciary's usurping the right of educators and publicly elected officials to make educational decisions. Those of us representing V.M.I. and the Commonwealth of Virginia believe that we met the tests that the Court had laid down in a similar case to determine when the government has a compelling interest in making gender distinctions. In ignoring our arguments, its own precedent, and the facts of the V.M.I. case, the Court overstepped its role as a check on legislative decision making and adopted its own view of social policy as constitutional law. Even those people who have no direct stake in the V.M.I. decision should be asking themselves whether the Court's decision, provides a sad omen for the future.

A Similar Previous Decision

The road to the V.M.I. decision began with Joe Hogan's short walk across his hometown of Columbus, Miss., and into the admissions office of the then-single-sex nursing program of the state-supported Mississippi University for Women. Mr. Hogan wished to avoid the 75-mile drive to a coed nursing program, but the state barred him from attending the university. In 1982, the Supreme Court considered his plea in a case known as *Mississippi University for Women v. Hogan*. The Court placed the burden on the university to justify Mr. Hogan's exclusion: To prevail, the institution had to show that its mission constituted a legitimate governmental objective, and that its single-sex admissions policy was substantially related to achieving that objective. The Court ruled that the university's argument—that it needed to exclude men from the nursing program to enhance opportunities for women, based on the rationale of affirmative action—made no sense in an occupation such as nursing, where women had never suffered a disadvantage.

V.M.I. and Virginia studied the tests established in *Hogan* carefully. In *Hogan*, the Court had criticized the Mississippi University for Women for not rethinking its charter since its founding in 1884. By contrast, well before the Justice Department sued V.M.I. in 1990 to force it to admit women, V.M.I. had appointed a committee to review its mission and admissions policy. To assure objectivity, V.M.I. made sure that the institute's graduates or those otherwise affiliated with it did not form a majority of the committee. After careful study, visits to the service academies at West Point and Annapolis to see how admitting women had affected them, and meetings with proponents of coeducation, the committee recommended in 1986 that V.M.I. continue its single-sex admissions policy. In the 1991 federal-court trial on the Justice Department's suit, a district judge found that the 1986 report constituted a "reasoned analysis" of V.M.I.'s mission and its single gender policy.

V.M.I.'s Unique Educational Methodology

V.M.I.'s mission is the development of educated men of character—men whose conduct is marked by honor, self-discipline, perseverance, and loyalty. While most colleges focus primarily or exclusively on the classroom and pay only lip service to such broader aspects of a liberal-arts education, V.M.I.'s educational approach is holistic, incorporating the barracks, the playing fields, and all aspects of life on the post. Indeed, unlike most colleges, where the library is the core educational facility, at V.M.I. the barracks serve as the focal point of the institute's educational program. Even government witnesses at the federal trial agreed that V.M.I.'s educational methodology rests on a holistic approach.

That methodology is based on treating all cadets alike and subjecting them to constant scrutiny and a total absence of privacy. This system is designed to insure that V.M.I. makes no distinctions among cadets, whether based on wealth, race, or intellect, and that all cadets comply with the same standards. At V.M.I. there are no locks, no curtains on the windows. Until their senior year, most cadets live in rooms with two or more other students; the rooms are so small that each day the beds are folded and placed against the wall at reveille [wake-up call] to make space for walking around.

Each cadet must endure a seven-month orientation known as "the rat line," which is an aggressive, student-administered, "adversative" model of discipline based on the old English public-school concept of physical and mental challenge. Knowledgeable experts compare the rat line to a boot camp run by the U. S. Marine Corps. The Corps conducts such camps separately for men and women, and V.M.I. also believes that its methodology requires separating men and women.

V.M.I. supporters do not contend that women are inherently unable to endure the rat line. But they do believe that homogeneity of gender is critical to the success of a program that treats all participants alike and subjects them to constant scrutiny. Moreover, aside from the demanding, broader aspects of the V.M.I. method, research has shown that some students—both men and women—benefit from single-gender educational classrooms.

By any measure, V.M.I.'S educational approach enables its graduates to achieve success far beyond expectations. Entering cadets at V.M.I. are largely young men of average ability, average background, and average economic means. Few National Merit Scholars enroll at V.M.I. Yet a recent Standard & Poor's survey ranked V.M.I. 30th among colleges and universities in the country in the number of graduates occupying leadership positions in American business. Many cadets readily acknowledge that they sought admission because they realized that they needed discipline or wanted the challenge of V.M.I.'s rigorous program. Most state that they wanted a single-gender educational experience. Interestingly, V.M.I. has a higher retention rate for African-American cadets than it does for white cadets. How many colleges can make such a boast?

Evidence in Support of V.M.I.

Some skeptics have argued that V.M.I.'s success comes from the prestige of its diploma and the help that graduates allegedly receive from its "network" of distinguished alumni. However, the Justice Department was unable to introduce a scintilla of evidence of such a network or its benefits. Indeed, were it real, the existence and use of such a network would be a perversion of V.M.I.'s principle that "you may be whatever you resolve to be" through perseverance and achievement.

It is undeniable that taking average students and producing superior graduates is a legitimate governmental objective. All society benefits from such a program. It is also undeniable that V.M.I.'s single-sex policy is substantially related to achieving its objective. All of the expert witnesses at the 1991 trial testified that the V.M.I. method would necessarily change if women were admitted, and the V.M.I. experts, whom the court found far more credible than those testifying against V.M.I., stated that V.M.I. could not achieve similar results in a coeducational environment. The federal district court judge and a panel of judges of the U.S. Court of Appeals for the Fourth Circuit said V.M.I. could keep its methodology and admissions policy if it set up a parallel program for women—which Virginia did, creating the Virginia Women's Institute for Leadership at nearby Mary Baldwin College.

Unable to rebut the overwhelming evidence supporting V.M.I.'s program, the majority of the Supreme Court chose simply to ignore it, along with the opinions of the lower courts. Indeed, as Justice Antonin Scalia suggested in a dissenting opinion, the parties could have saved the expense and effort of a trial, for all the attention that the majority paid to the evidence in the record.

Moreover, the Court was so eager to set its own policy that it laid down a confusing precedent for the future. Even *The Washington Post* editorial page (which welcomed the result) recognized that the Court's reasoning made it difficult to predict the impact of its ruling. Previously, public institutions making gender distinctions had only to meet the two-part standard laid down in *Hogan*: demonstrating a legitimate objective and showing that the gender distinctions were substantially related to achieving that objective. Now, in addition, the Court says that the justification must be "exceedingly persuasive" and that it will be viewed with "skeptical scrutiny." The skeptical-scrutiny standard gives the Court leeway to second-guess with impunity and discredit the "reasoned analysis" of state and local governments, educators, and regulators.

Overstepping by the Court

The Court also refused to address the benefits of single-gender education, which, at least in the public sector, it relegated to the trash heap without recognizing that many students benefit from it and prefer it to coeducation. Surely no one can contend that coeducation in America is so universally successful that we can afford to dump, under the guise of civil liberty for a few, a method of education that has worked well for so many. In Virginia, V.M.I.'s single-sex program adds to a diversity of educational offerings that includes the new program set up with state funds at Mary Baldwin College, four private women's colleges (whose students receive state tuition grants), and a coed military program for cadets at Virginia Polytechnic Institute and State University. In addition, the Court ignored the unwillingness of Congress to eliminate an exemption for single-sex public and private colleges and universities in Title IX of the Education Amendments of 1972.

What *does* this decision augur for the future of appellate review and the development of constitutional law? We should all be concerned by the majority's willingness in the V.M.I.

case to ignore the evidence in the record, its own precedent, and Congress. We should worry about its willingness to apply a new standard of scrutiny to invalidate the reasoned analysis of state educational decisions. We should be dismayed by the Court's eagerness to substitute its own educational views for those of experts far more knowledgeable on the subject.

When the Supreme Court disregards the record of a case and its own precedent to reach a particular result, as it did in the V.M.I. case, it acts as a legislature, not a judiciary. The genius of our tripartite [three-part] form of government is that the judiciary is supposed to act as a check on legislative power, not as a substitute for it. Under our Constitution, only those answerable to the people are empowered to make social policy for us. The Supreme Court's decision challenges that democratic precept on which our republic is based.

> *"Despite the continuing uncertainty of the legal status of single-sex programs in public schools, many school districts nationwide have read the new Title IX regulations as a green light to segregate."*

The Legal Status of Single-Sex Programs in Public Schools Is Uncertain

Ariela Migdal, Emily J. Martin, Mie Lewis, and Lenora M. Lapidus

Lenora M. Lapidus is director, Emily J. Martin deputy director, and Ariela Migdal and Mie Lewis staff attorneys of the Women's Rights Project of the American Civil Liberties Union.

In the following article, Migdal, Martin, Lewis, and Lapidus discuss the uncertain legal status of single-sex schools and classes in public schools. The authors claim that the increasing popularity of sex-segregated education is driven by theories of gender differences between boys and girls, but they contend that no evidence shows that students do better in a single-sex setting. The authors claim that little case precedent regarding single-sex education and recent changes to Title IX permitting sex-segregated classes have resulted in an increase in sex-segregated programs around the country. The authors claim that some federal laws

Ariela Migdal, Emily J. Martin, Mie Lewis, and Lenora M. Lapidus, "The Need to Address Equal Educational Opportunities for Women and Girls," *Human Rights*, vol. 35, Summer 2008, pp. 16–19.
Copyright © 2008, American Bar Association. All rights reserved. Reprinted with permission. This information or any portion thereof may not be copied or disseminated in any form or by any means or stored in an electronic database or retrieval system without the express written consent of the American Bar Association.

146

and legal precedent support a limit to sex-segregation in public schools, including the 1996 case of United States v. Virginia, *wherein the Supreme Court determined that the male-only admissions policy of a state university violated the equal protection clause of the Fourteenth Amendment.*

While all students are vulnerable to assaults on their rights, girls and women face a distinct set of challenges. This article . . . addresses the current popularity of sex-segregated programs in public schools, in which boys and girls are taught differently in curricula based on gender stereotypes that traditionally have been used to limit girls' opportunities. . . .

New Push for Sex-Segregated Schools

Today, more and more public school districts separate girls from boys. According to the National Association for Single-Sex Public Education (NASSPE), a leading proponent of sex-segregated programs, while only four sex-segregated public schools existed in the country a decade ago, today there are approximately four hundred. A sex segregation movement is successfully pushing to increase this number, recently amending laws in Michigan, Wisconsin, Delaware, and Florida to foster the creation of sex-segregated programs in public schools. This trend is accelerating in the wake of the federal Department of Education's (DOE) 2006 revision of a long-standing regulation to permit sex-segregated classes in coeducational schools receiving federal funding.

An increasingly popular rationale for separating boys and girls in school is the notion that boys' and girls' brains are so different that they cannot both succeed in the same classroom. Two influential proponents of this theory are the writers Leonard Sax and Michael Gurian. Sax is a psychologist and the director of NASSPE; Gurian is a counselor and corporate consultant with a graduate degree in creative writing, as well as founder of the Gurian Institute, which conducts trainings on brain differences between the sexes. Both Sax and the Gurian Institute are in the business of training teachers from public school districts across the country. Many of those teaching single-sex classes rely on their theories and methods.

Theories of Gender Differences

While Sax and Gurian concede that not all boys or all girls are the same, they attempt to prove that, as the title of one of Gurian's books proclaims, *Boys and Girls Learn Differently!*, and they argue that teachers should treat boys and girls differently as a result. For example, Sax claims that teachers should smile at girls and look them in the eye but must not look boys directly in the eye or smile at them. He claims that boys do well under stress, while girls do badly. As a result, according to Sax, girls should never be given time limits on tests and should be encouraged to take their shoes off in class because this helps them relax and think. Sax also claims that girls will do better in school if they are allowed to bring blankets from home to cuddle in during class time. Sax argues that any boy who likes to read, does not enjoy contact sports, and does not have a lot of close male friends should be firmly disciplined, required to spend time with "normal males" and made to play sports. Gurian propounds similar theories, including that boys are better than girls in math because their bodies receive daily surges of testosterone, while girls have equivalent mathematics skills only during the few days in their menstrual cycle when they have an estrogen surge.

These theories have a real world impact in schools. David Chadwell, a member of the board of directors of NASSPE, directs the Office of Single-Gender Initiatives in the South Carolina Department of Education. South Carolina has more sex-segregated schools and classes than any other state in the country, a trend Chadwell encourages by publicizing sample lesson plans emphasizing physical activity, competition, and technology in classes for boys and friendship, team building, decorating assignments and projects, and stress reduction in classes for girls.

Most proponents of single-sex education argue that segregation leads to greater academic achievement. Yet no compelling, consistent evidence supports this conclusion. Some studies find that students in coeducational schools do better than students in single-sex schools. Other studies find the opposite. The bulk of studies show no difference between the two in terms of student achievement. In fact, in 2005 the DOE [Department of Education] published an extensive review of existing studies and characterized the data as "equivocal." In other words, it found no clear evidence showing that, in general, students are more likely to succeed in single-sex schools.

The Change to Title IX

Few cases have yet challenged sex segregation in public elementary and secondary schools, probably because, until recently, such segregation was rare in the thirty-six years since the passage of Title IX of the Education Amendments of 1972, the federal law prohibiting sex discrimination in federally funded education. With narrow exceptions for activities such as father-son activities and beauty pageants, Title IX states, "No person in the United States shall, on the basis of sex, be excluded from participation in, be denied the benefits of, or be subjected to discrimination under any education program or activity receiving Federal financial assistance." For more than thirty years, DOE regulations implementing Title IX had interpreted the statute to prohibit coeducational schools from segregating students by sex in almost all circumstances, with exceptions for sex education and contact sports.

In 2006, however, the DOE revised its Title IX regulations to permit coeducational schools to offer sex-segregated classes. The new regulations allow a school to create sex-segregated classes or extracurricular activities either to provide "diverse" educational options to students or to address what the school has judged to be students' particular educational needs. The regulations make clear, however, that participation in a sex-segregated class must be completely voluntary and explain that participation is not completely voluntary unless a "substantially equal" coeducational class is offered in the same subject.

Legal Status of Single-Sex Programs

The DOE's regulatory change, however, does not affect other laws limiting sex segregation in public schools. First, other federal agencies funding educational programs and activities have regulations prohibiting sex-segregated classes; thus, for example, school districts that receive U.S. Department of Agriculture funding for school lunch programs are presumably bound by its regulations prohibiting sex segregation. Second, the U.S. Supreme Court has made clear that at least some single-sex programs violate the Equal Protection Clause of the U.S. Constitution, striking down both the Virginia Military Institute's men-only policy and Mississippi University for Women's women-only policy as unconstitutionally discriminatory. The Court warned that public schools attempting to justify sex-segregated programs shoulder a heavy burden of persuasion and made clear that generalizations about average differences in the pedagogical needs of women and men do not justify excluding members of one sex from a unique educational opportunity. Third, the federal Equal Educational Opportunities Act prohibits assigning students to single-sex schools.

Based on conflicts between the 2006 DOE regulations and the requirements of Title IX and the Constitution, the American Civil Liberties Union has recently challenged the validity of these regulations in federal court; the legality of the regulations likely will be litigated in coming months. Despite the continuing uncertainty of the legal status of single-sex programs in public schools, many school districts nationwide have read the new Title IX regulations as a green light to segregate. As a result, more and more programs are being crafted throughout the country based on the notion that boys and girls require very different kinds of education—a theory that by definition will introduce sharp sex-based inequalities to the public schools.

CHAPTER 4

Gender-Based Discrimination Toward Transsexuals Is Sex Discrimination

Case Overview

Smith v. Salem, Ohio, et al. (2004)

In *Smith v. Salem, Ohio, et al.*, the U.S. Court of Appeals for the Sixth District ruled that a transsexual who had been subjected to sex stereotyping based on nonconforming gender behavior was the victim of sex discrimination. Title VII of the Civil Rights Act of 1964 prohibits discrimination by employers on the basis of sex, among other things. In *Price Waterhouse v. Hopkins* (1989), the U.S. Supreme Court determined that sex stereotyping could constitute discrimination based on sex under Title VII. In *Smith*, the appeals court determined that sex stereotyping of a transsexual is no more permissible than that of a nontranssexual, as the key prohibited behavior under Title VII is discrimination based on expectations of gender behavior.

Jimmie L. Smith was a lieutenant in the Salem, Ohio, fire department. He was born a biological male but was diagnosed with gender identity disorder, a disorder that the American Psychiatric Association characterizes as a long-standing and strong identification with another gender that causes significant impairment in an individual's life. After seven years at the fire department Smith began to dress and act more feminine and, after being asked about his transgendered behavior, informed his supervisor of his condition and of the likelihood that he would eventually make a full physical transition from male to female. Shortly thereafter, the city's executive body held a meeting to plan Smith's termination. Smith was notified that he would be required to undergo three psychological evaluations by doctors chosen by the city and, after refusing and threatening to sue, was suspended from work.

Smith filed suit in the federal district court alleging sex discrimination under Title VII. The district court dismissed his claims.

Smith appealed his case to the U.S. Court of Appeals for the Sixth District, which reversed the district court's holding. The court determined that Smith was able to sue under Title VII, finding the treatment of Smith to be covered by Title VII's prohibition of discrimination based on sex. The court also determined that Smith had succeeded in stating a claim for sex stereotyping relevant to the U.S. Supreme Court's decision in *Price Waterhouse v. Hopkins* (1989), which determined that sex stereotyping constitutes sex discrimination under Title VII. The U.S. Court of Appeals for the Sixth District rejected the district court's claim that transsexuals are not entitled to Title VII protection, noting that the decision in *Price Waterhouse* had extended the original understanding of sex discrimination under Title VII to also encompass gender discrimination. Thus, the court concluded, employers may not discriminate against employees for gender nonconformity by males or females; thus, Smith was the victim of sex discrimination.

There is no federal law that explicitly prohibits discrimination against transsexuals or transgendered persons. The issue considered by the U.S. Court of Appeals for the Sixth District in *Smith* regarding discrimination of transsexuals has not yet appeared before the U.S. Supreme Court. Several lower courts and other circuit courts, however, have found that Title VII's protection against sex discrimination does not apply to transsexual and transgender discrimination. In the coming years, the U.S. Supreme Court is likely to hear a case on this issue, making a more certain determination about whether or not laws prohibiting sex discrimination apply to the discrimination of transsexuals and transgendered persons.

"Sex stereotyping based on a person's gender-non-conforming behavior is impermissible discrimination, irrespective of the cause of that behavior."

The Court's Decision: Gender Stereotyping of Transsexuals in Employment Decisions Is Discriminatory

R. Guy Cole Jr.

R. Guy Cole Jr. is a judge for the U.S. Court of Appeals for the Sixth Circuit, the federal appeals court for Kentucky, Michigan, Ohio, and Tennessee.

The following is excerpted from the 2004 U.S. Court of Appeals for the Sixth District case of Smith v. Salem, Ohio, et al., *in which the court ruled that Jimmie L. Smith, a transsexual who had been subjected to sex stereotyping based on nonconforming gender behavior, was the victim of sex discrimination. Title VII of the Civil Rights Act of 1964 prohibits discrimination by employers on the basis of sex, among other things. In* Price Waterhouse v. Hopkins *(1989), the U.S. Supreme Court determined that sex stereotyping could constitute discrimination based on sex under Title VII. In* Smith, *the appeals court determined that sex stereotyping of a transsexual is no more permissible than that of a nontranssexual, as the key prohibited behavior under Title VII is discrimination based on expectations of gender behavior.*

R. Guy Cole Jr., majority opinion, *Smith v. Salem, Ohio, et al.*, U.S. Court of Appeals for the Sixth District, August 5, 2004.

Smith is—and has been, at all times relevant to this action—employed by the city of Salem, Ohio, as a lieutenant in the Salem Fire Department (the "Fire Department"). Prior to the events surrounding this action, Smith worked for the Fire Department for seven years without any negative incidents. Smith—biologically and by birth a male—is a transsexual and has been diagnosed with Gender Identity Disorder ("GID"), which the American Psychiatric Association characterizes as a disjunction between an individual's sexual organs and sexual identity. After being diagnosed with GID, Smith began "expressing a more feminine appearance on a full-time basis"—including at work—in accordance with international medical protocols for treating GID. Soon thereafter, Smith's co-workers began questioning him about his appearance and commenting that his appearance and mannerisms were not "masculine enough." As a result, Smith notified his immediate supervisor, Defendant Thomas Eastek, about his GID diagnosis and treatment. He also informed Eastek of the likelihood that his treatment would eventually include complete physical transformation from male to female. Smith had approached Eastek in order to answer any questions Eastek might have concerning his appearance and manner and so that Eastek could address Smith's co-workers' comments and inquiries. Smith specifically asked Eastek, and Eastek promised, not to divulge the substance of their conversation to any of his superiors, particularly to Defendant Walter Greenamyer, Chief of the Fire Department. In short order, however, Eastek told Greenamyer about Smith's behavior and his GID.

Meeting on Smith's Employment

Greenamyer then met with Defendant C. Brooke Zellers, the Law Director for the City of Salem, with the intention of using Smith's transsexualism and its manifestations as a basis for terminating his employment. On April 18, 2001, Greenamyer and Zellers arranged a meeting of the City's executive body to discuss Smith and devise a plan for terminating his employment. The executive body included Defendants Larry D. DeJane, Salem's mayor; James A. Armeni, Salem's auditor; and Joseph S. Julian, Salem's service director. Also present was Salem Safety Director Henry L. Willard, now deceased, who was never a named defendant in this action.

Although Ohio Revised Code § 121.22(G)—which sets forth the state procedures pursuant to which Ohio municipal officials may meet to take employment action against a municipal employee—provides that officials "may hold an executive session to consider the appointment, employment, dismissal, discipline, promotion, demotion, or compensation of a public employee only after a majority of a quorum of the public body determines, by a roll call vote, to hold an executive session and only at a regular or special meeting for the sole purpose of [considering such matters]," the City did not abide by these procedures at the April 18, 2001, meeting.

During the meeting, Greenamyer, DeJane, and Zellers agreed to arrange for the Salem Civil Service Commission to require Smith to undergo three separate psychological evaluations with physicians of the City's choosing. They hoped that Smith would either resign or refuse to comply. If he refused to comply, Defendants reasoned, they could terminate Smith's employment on the ground of insubordination. Willard, who remained silent during the meeting, telephoned Smith afterwards to inform him of the plan, calling Defendants' scheme a "witch hunt."

Smith's Suspension and Complaint

Two days after the meeting, on April 20, 2001, Smith's counsel telephoned DeJane to advise him of Smith's legal representation and the potential legal ramifications for the City if it followed through on the plan devised by Defendants during the April 18 meeting. On April 22, 2001, Smith received his "right to sue" letter from the U.S. Equal Employment Opportunity

Commission ("EEOC"). Four days after that, on April 26, 2001, Greenamyer suspended Smith for one twenty-four hour shift, based on his alleged infraction of a City and/or Fire Department policy.

At a subsequent hearing before the Salem Civil Service Commission (the "Commission") regarding his suspension, Smith contended that the suspension was a result of selective enforcement in retaliation for his having obtained legal representation in response to Defendants' plan to terminate his employment because of his transsexualism and its manifestations. At the hearing, Smith sought to elicit testimony from witnesses regarding the meeting of April 18, 2001, but the City objected and the Commission's chairman, Defendant Harry Dugan, refused to allow any testimony regarding the meeting, despite the fact that Ohio Administrative Code § 124-9-11 permitted Smith to introduce evidence of disparate treatment and selective enforcement in his hearing before the Commission.

The Commission ultimately upheld Smith's suspension. Smith appealed to the Columbiana County Court of Common Pleas, which reversed the suspension, finding that "[b]ecause the regulation [that Smith was alleged to have violated] was not effective[,] [Smith] could not be charged with violation of it."

Smith then filed suit in the federal district court. In his complaint, he asserted Title VII claims of sex discrimination and retaliation, along with claims pursuant to 42 U.S.C. [United States Code] § 1983 and state law claims of invasion of privacy and civil conspiracy. In a Memorandum Opinion and Order dated February 26, 2003, the district court dismissed the federal claims and granted judgment on the pleadings to Defendants pursuant to Federal Rule of Civil Procedure 12(c). The district judge also dismissed the state law claims without prejudice, having declined to exercise supplemental jurisdiction over them pursuant to 28 U.S.C. § 1367(c)(3). . . .

Smith's Title VII Claims

The parties disagree over two issues pertaining to Smith's Title VII claims: (1) whether Smith properly alleged a claim of sex stereotyping, in violation of the Supreme Court's pronouncements in *Price Waterhouse v. Hopkins* (1989); and (2) whether Smith alleged that he suffered an adverse employment action.

Defendants do not challenge Smith's complaint with respect to any of the other elements necessary to establish discrimination and retaliation claims pursuant to Title VII. In any event, we affirmatively find that Smith has made out a *prima facie* [apparent] case for both claims. To establish a *prima facie* case of employment discrimination pursuant to Title VII, Smith must show that: (1) he is a member of a protected class; (2) he suffered an adverse employment action; (3) he was qualified for the position in question; and (4) he was treated differently from similarly situated individuals outside of his protected class. Smith is a member of a protected class. His complaint asserts that he is a male with Gender Identity Disorder, and Title VII's prohibition of discrimination "because of . . . sex" protects men as well as women. The complaint also alleges both that Smith was qualified for the position in question—he had been a lieutenant in the Fire Department for seven years without any negative incidents—and that he would not have been treated differently, on account of his non-masculine behavior and GID, had he been a woman instead of a man.

To establish a *prima facie* case of retaliation pursuant to Title VII, a plaintiff must show that: (1) he engaged in an activity protected by Title VII; (2) the defendant knew he engaged in this protected activity; (3) thereafter, the defendant took an employment action adverse to him; and (4) there was a causal connection between the protected activity and the adverse employment action. Smith's complaint satisfies the first two requirements by explaining how he sought legal counsel after learning of the Salem executive body's April 18, 2001, meeting concerning his employment; how his attorney contacted Defendant DeJane to advise Defendants of Smith's representation; and how Smith filed a complaint with the EEOC concerning Defendants' meeting and intended actions. With respect to the fourth requirement, a causal connection between the protected activity and the adverse employment action, "[a]lthough no one factor is dispositive in establishing a causal connection, evidence . . . that the adverse action was taken shortly after the plaintiff's exercise of protected rights is relevant to causation" [*Nguyen v. City of Cleveland* (6th Cir. 2000)]. Here, Smith was suspended on April 26, 2001, just days after he engaged in protected activity by receiving his "right to sue" letter from the EEOC, which occurred four days before the suspension, and by his attorney contacting Mayor DeJane, which occurred six days before the suspension. The temporal proximity between the events is significant enough to constitute direct evidence of a causal connection for the purpose of satisfying Smith's burden of demonstrating a *prima facie* case.

We turn now to examining whether Smith properly alleged a claim of sex stereotyping, in violation of the Supreme Court's pronouncements in *Price Waterhouse v. Hopkins*, and whether Smith alleged that he suffered an adverse employment action.

The Claim of Sex Stereotyping

Title VII of the Civil Rights Act of 1964 provides, in relevant part, that "[i]t shall be an unlawful employment practice for an employer . . . to discriminate against any individual with respect to his compensation, terms, conditions, or privileges of employment because of such individual's race, color, religion, sex, or national origin."

In his complaint, Smith asserts Title VII claims of retaliation and employment discrimination "because of . . . sex." The district court dismissed Smith's Title VII claims on the ground that he failed to state a claim for sex stereotyping pursuant to *Price Waterhouse v. Hopkins.* The district court implied that Smith's claim was disingenuous, stating that he merely "invokes the term-of-art created by *Price Waterhouse,* that is, 'sex-stereotyping,'" as an end run around his "real" claim, which, the district court stated, was "based upon his transsexuality." The district court then held that "Title VII does not prohibit discrimination based on an individual's transsexualism."

Relying on *Price Waterhouse*—which held that Title VII's prohibition of discrimination "because of . . . sex" bars gender discrimination, including discrimination based on sex stereotypes—Smith contends on appeal that he was a victim of discrimination "because of . . . sex" both because of his gender-non-conforming conduct and, more generally, because of his identification as a transsexual.

We first address whether Smith has stated a claim for relief, pursuant to *Price Waterhouse's* prohibition of sex stereotyping, based on his gender-non-conforming behavior and appearance. In *Price Waterhouse,* the plaintiff, a female senior manager in an accounting firm, was denied partnership in the firm, in part, because she was considered "macho." She was advised that she could improve her chances for partnership if she were to take "a course at charm school," "walk more femininely, talk more femininely, dress more femininely, wear make-up, have her hair styled, and wear jewelry." Six members of the Court agreed that such comments bespoke gender discrimination, holding that Title VII barred not just discrimination because Hopkins was a woman, but also sex stereotyping—that is, discrimination because she failed to *act* like a woman. As Judge [Richard A.] Posner has pointed out, the term "gender" is one "borrowed from grammar to designate the sexes as viewed as social rather than biological classes." The Supreme Court made clear that in the context of Title VII, discrimination because of "sex" includes gender discrimination: "In the context of sex stereotyping, an employer who acts on the basis of a belief that a woman cannot be aggressive, or that she must not be, has acted on the basis of gender." The Court emphasized that "we are beyond the day when an employer could evaluate employees by assuming or insisting that they matched the stereotype associated with their group."

A Case of Discrimination

Smith contends that the same theory of sex stereotyping applies here. His complaint sets forth the conduct and mannerisms which, he alleges, did not conform with his employers' and co-workers' sex stereotypes of how a man should look and behave. Smith's complaint states that, after being diagnosed with GID, he began to express a more feminine appearance and manner on a regular basis, including at work. The complaint states that his co-workers began commenting on his appearance and mannerisms as not being masculine enough; and that his supervisors at the Fire Department and other municipal agents knew about this allegedly unmasculine conduct and appearance. The complaint then describes a high-level meeting among Smith's supervisors and other municipal officials regarding his employment. Defendants allegedly schemed to compel Smith's resignation by forcing him to undergo multiple psychological evaluations of his gender-nonconforming behavior. The complaint makes clear that these meetings took place soon after Smith assumed a more feminine appearance and manner and after his conversation about this with Eastek. In addition, the complaint alleges that Smith was suspended for twenty-four hours for allegedly violating an unenacted municipal policy, and that the suspension was ordered in retaliation for his pursuing legal remedies after he had been informed about Defendants' plan to intimidate him into resigning. In short, Smith claims that the discrimination he experienced was based on his failure to conform to sex stereotypes by expressing less masculine, and more feminine mannerisms and appearance.

Having alleged that his failure to conform to sex stereotypes concerning how a man should look and behave was the driving force behind Defendants' actions, Smith has sufficiently pleaded claims of sex stereotyping and gender discrimination. . . .

After *Price Waterhouse*, an employer who discriminates against women because, for instance, they do not wear dresses or makeup, is engaging in sex discrimination because the discrimination would not occur but for the victim's sex. It follows that employers who discriminate against men because they *do* wear dresses and makeup, or otherwise act femininely, are also engaging in sex discrimination, because the discrimination would not occur but for the victim's sex.

Discrimination of Transsexuals

Yet some courts have held that this latter form of discrimination is of a different and somehow more permissible kind. For instance, the man who acts in ways typically associated with women is not described as engaging in the same activity as a woman who acts in ways typically associated with women, but is instead described as engaging in the different activity of being a transsexual (or in some instances, a homosexual or transvestite). Discrimination against the transsexual is then found not to be discrimination "because of . . . sex," but rather, discrimination against the plaintiff's unprotected status or mode of self-identification. In other words, these courts superimpose classifications such as "transsexual" on a plaintiff, and then legitimize discrimination based on the plaintiff's gender-non-conformity by formalizing the non-conformity into an ostensibly unprotected classification.

Such was the case here: despite the fact that Smith alleges that Defendants' discrimination was motivated by his appearance and mannerisms, which Defendants felt were inappropriate for his perceived sex, the district court expressly declined to discuss the applicability of *Price Waterhouse*. The district court therefore gave insufficient consideration to Smith's well-pleaded claims concerning his contra-gender behavior, but rather accounted for that behavior only insofar as it confirmed for the court Smith's status as a transsexual, which the district court held precluded Smith from Title VII protection.

Such analyses cannot be reconciled with *Price Waterhouse*, which does not make Title VII protection against sex stereotyping conditional or provide any reason to exclude Title VII coverage for non sex-stereotypical behavior simply because the person is a transsexual. As such, discrimination against a plaintiff who is a transsexual—and therefore fails to act and/or identify with his or her gender—is no different from the discrimination directed against Ann Hopkins in *Price Waterhouse*, who, in sex-stereotypical terms, did not act like a woman. Sex stereotyping based on a person's gender-nonconforming behavior is impermissible discrimination, irrespective of the cause of that behavior; a label, such as "transsexual," is not fatal to a sex discrimination claim where the victim has suffered discrimination because of his or her gender-non-conformity. Accordingly, we hold that Smith has stated a claim for relief pursuant to Title VII's prohibition of sex discrimination. . . .

Discrimination and Retaliation

Common to both the employment discrimination and retaliation claims is a showing of an adverse employment action, which is defined as a "materially adverse change in the terms and conditions of [plaintiff's] employment" [*Hollins v. Atlantic Co.* (6th Cir. 1999)]. A "bruised ego," a "mere inconvenience or an alteration of job responsibilities" is not enough to constitute an adverse employment action [*White v. Burlington Northern & Santa Fe Ry. Co.* (6th Cir. 2002)]. Examples of adverse employment actions include firing, failing to promote, reassignment with significantly different responsibilities, a material loss of benefits, suspensions, and other indices unique to a particular situation. Here, the Fire Department suspended Smith for twenty-four hours. Because Smith works in twenty-four hour shifts, that twenty-four hour suspension was the equivalent of three eight-hour days for the average worker, or, approximately 60% of a forty-hour work week. Pursuant to the liberal notice pleading requirements set forth in Fed. R. Civ. P. 8, this allegation, at this phase of the litigation, is sufficient to satisfy the adverse employment requirement of both an employment discrimination and retaliation claim pursuant to Title VII. . . .

Accordingly, Smith has stated an adverse employment action and, therefore, satisfied all of the elements necessary to allege a *prima facie* case of employment discrimination and retaliation pursuant to Title VII. We therefore reverse the district court's grant of judgment on the pleadings to Defendants with respect to those claims.

> *"There is still resistance from some federal courts that perceive lawsuits relying on* Smith *to be artful pleadings."*

Courts Are Still Divided About Transsexual Rights After *Smith*

Dee McAree

Dee McAree is a staff reporter for the National Law Journal.

In the following article, McAree reports that not all courts are following the precedent set by the U.S. Court of Appeals for the Sixth District in Smith v. Salem, Ohio, et al., *which found that transsexuals who are the victims of sex stereotyping in employment decisions are protected by Title VII of the 1964 Civil Rights Act. McAree points to disagreements in district courts and the courts of appeal on the issue, finding that some courts after* Smith *have applied older precedents to transsexual discrimination lawsuits, determining that Title VII does not protect transsexuals. McAree concludes that if agreement is not reached in the circuit courts, the issue could likely one day head to the U.S. Supreme Court.*

A ground-breaking decision by the 6th U.S. Circuit Court of Appeals opened doors for transsexuals to bring discrimination lawsuits against their employers, but some lower federal courts are still holding to older precedents that bar Title VII claims.

"District court judges are having a hard time with this," said Christopher Daley, a lawyer and director of the Transgender Law Center in San Francisco. "They are having a hard time feeling that they can really embrace the 6th Circuit ruling."

Sex Discrimination Under Title VII

Traditionally, federal courts have denied that transsexuals are a protected class under Title VII of the 1964 Civil Rights Act, based on a strict reading of how Congress intended the term "sex" to be applied. They hold to a line of cases that stem from a 1984 7th Circuit ruling, *Ulane v. Eastern Airlines Inc.*, 742 F.2d 1081, which reinforced a narrow reading of Title VII.

The 6th Circuit, however, broke new ground in 2004 when it relied on a 1989 U.S. Supreme Court decision in *Price Waterhouse v. Hopkins*, 490 U.S. 228, to find that transsexuals can be victims of sexual stereotyping. *Price Waterhouse* dealt with a woman passed over for promotion because she did not act as feminine as her employer required. In *Smith v. City of Salem*, No. 03-3399, the 6th Circuit said the same reasoning can apply to a transsexual firefighter who does not appear masculine enough.

Disagreement in the Courts

Yet as recently as last month, a federal judge rejected the 6th Circuit decision in favor of older precedent.

Senior Judge David Sam of U.S. district court in Utah, which is within the 10th Circuit, rejected the employment discrimination claims of a transsexual bus driver.

"The Sixth Circuit, in two recent cases, has applied the *Price Waterhouse* rationale to transsexuals, and has concluded that *Ulane* and its progeny are no longer good law.... This court disagrees," Sam wrote, *Etsitty v. Utah Transit Authority*, No. 2.04CV616 DS (D. Utah).

Major Implications

Attorney Randi Barnabee of Smith Barnabee & Co. in North-field, Ohio, who argued *Smith*, said she knew when she first read *Price Waterhouse* in law school that the case would have implications for transsexuals.

"I thought 'this is the case that is going to change everything,'" said Barnabee. Discrimination against homosexuals or transsexuals is always triggered by the perception that they do not conform to either sex, she claimed. But there is still resistance from some federal courts that perceive lawsuits relying on *Smith* to be artful pleadings that are trying to circumvent *Ulane*, Barnabee said.

With an appeal in the *Etsitty* case headed for the 10th Circuit, lawyers expect to see more clarity in the law.

"Either the circuits are going to get in line behind *Smith* or they are going to split," Daley said. If the circuits split, it may well be an issue headed for the U.S. Supreme Court, he added.

Sex Stereotyping After *Price Waterhouse*

Many of the cases involving Title VII claims by transsexuals, like *Etsitty*, involve restroom issues, where an employer fires a transsexual employee over concerns about which restroom will be used.

Lauren Scholnick of Strindberg Scholnick & Chamness, who is representing Utah plaintiff Krystal Etsitty, said that the restroom issue is only a pretext for the employers' discomfort with their employee's gender nonconformity.

"It's very clear after *Price Waterhouse* that employers have a duty to protect their employees [from discrimination based on sex-stereotyping]," Scholnick said.

Defense lawyers have argued, with some success, that *Smith* creates another protected class for transsexuals and homosexuals, in opposition to *Ulane*.

Scott Hagen of Ray Quinney & Nebeker in Salt Lake City, who defended the Utah Transit Authority in *Etsitty*, declined to discuss the case while an appeal is still pending.

But in *Etsitty*, Sam sided with the defense argument that the *Price Waterhouse* scenario of a woman appearing too masculine is not analogous to the case of a man changing to the opposite sex.

"There appears to be a growing trend toward recognizing a cause of action for sex discrimination under Title VII when a transgender person suffers an adverse employment action."

Smith Reflects a Trend Toward Protecting the Rights of Transgender Persons

John P. Furfaro and Risa M. Salins

John P. Furfaro is a partner and Risa M. Salins an associate at the law firm of Skadden, Arps, Slate, Meagher & Flom in New York City.

In the following article, Furfaro and Salins recount the historical treatment of claims of gender discrimination, arguing that there has been a recent movement toward more protection for transgender persons. They claim that the early understanding of sex discrimination prohibited under Title VII of the Civil Rights Act of 1965 was not applied to discrimination of transgender persons. After the 1989 Supreme Court case of Price Waterhouse v. Hopkins, *they contend, lower courts began to apply the protections of Title VII to transgender persons. Among the cases they discuss is* Smith v. Salem, Ohio, et al., *wherein the U.S. Court of Appeals for the Sixth District found that transsexuals who are the victims of sex stereotyping in employment decisions are protected by Title VII of the 1964 Civil Rights Act.*

On June 17, 2007, New Jersey [became] one of a growing number of states, including California, Illinois, Maine, Minnesota, New Mexico, Rhode Island and Washington, with a law expressly prohibiting employment discrimination on the basis of gender identity.

An even greater number of local statutes and ordinances, including the New York City Human Rights Law, expressly protect transgender persons against discrimination based on gender identity. However, there is presently no federal law that explicitly provides such protection to transgender persons. Title VII of the Civil Rights Act of 1964 prohibits employers from discriminating against any individual "because of . . . sex," 42 USC §2000e-2, but does not specifically mention sexual orientation or gender identity.

Federal courts have traditionally held that discrimination on the basis of an individual's transgender status, like discrimination based on sexual orientation, is not discrimination "because of sex" and is therefore not prohibited under Title VII. However, there appears to be a growing trend toward recognizing a cause of action for sex discrimination under Title VII when a transgender person suffers an adverse employment action. This development is grounded in the U.S. Supreme Court's decision in *Price Waterhouse v. Hopkins* 420 US 228 (1989), a case which found that discrimination based on a failure to conform to stereotypical gender norms—so-called "sex stereotyping"—can violate Title VII.

This [viewpoint] describes the historical treatment of claims of transgender discrimination and explains the recent movement toward greater protection for transgender persons under Title VII.

Early Understanding of Sex Discrimination

Prior courts have held that transgender individuals have no recourse against employment discrimination under Title VII. For example, in 1977, the U.S. Court of Appeals for the Ninth

Circuit in *Holloway v. Arthur Andersen*, 566 F2d 659 (9th Cir 1977), affirmed the district court's dismissal of Ramona Holloway's Title VII claim that she was fired for her transsexuality because "transexualism was not encompassed with the definition of 'sex' as the term appears in [Title VII]." Ms. Holloway worked for Arthur Anderson for five years, received a promotion and then was terminated shortly after informing her supervisor that she was undergoing treatment in preparation for sex-change surgery and changing her name from Robert to Ramona. In rejecting her claim, the Ninth Circuit looked to the legislative history of Title VII and found that its sex-discrimination provisions "were intended to place women on an equal footing with men." Since Congress had not shown any intent other than to restrict the term "sex" to its traditional meaning, the court would not expand Title VII's protection in the absence of a congressional mandate.

Similarly, in *Ulane v. Eastern Airlines Inc.* 742 F2d 1081 (7th Cir 1984), the U.S. Court of Appeals for Seventh Circuit rejected a Title VII claim brought by a transsexual pilot who was terminated after transitioning from male to female, holding that "[t]he words of Title VII do not outlaw discrimination against a person who has a sexual identity disorder." The court explained that the phrase in Title VII prohibiting discrimination based on sex, in its plain meaning, implies that "it is unlawful to discriminate against women because they are women and against men because they are men."

The Issue of Sex Stereotyping

Five years after *Ulane*, in the groundbreaking case of *Price Waterhouse v. Hopkins*, the U.S. Supreme Court introduced the notion of "sex stereotyping" as the basis for framing a sex discrimination claim under Title VII. Specifically, the *Price Waterhouse* Court held that Title VII is not limited to discrimination on the basis of one's biological status as a man or a woman but instead prohibits the "entire spectrum" of discrimination on the basis of sex, including discrimination on the basis of sex stereotypes. The plaintiff Ann Hopkins sued Price Waterhouse for sex discrimination under Title VII after she was denied partnership because she failed to meet the firm's expectations about how a woman should look and act.

For example, Ms. Hopkins was told she should "walk more femininely, talk more femininely, dress more femininely, wear make-up, have her hair styled, and wear jewelry." The Supreme Court adopted the district court's finding that Price Waterhouse unlawfully discriminated against Hopkins on the basis of sex by "consciously giving credence and effect" to partners' comments that resulted from "an impermissibly cabined view of the proper behavior of women." The Court rejected Price Waterhouse's argument that Title VII did not prohibit discrimination based on gender stereotypes, declaring: "[W]e are beyond the day when an employer could evaluate employees by assuming or insisting that they matched the stereotype associated with their group, for 'in forbidding employers to discriminate against individuals because of their sex, Congress intended to strike at the entire spectrum of disparate treatment of men and women resulting from sex stereotypes.'"

Protection for Transgender Persons

Notably, *Price Waterhouse* did not involve a transgender plaintiff, but rather a female employee who was considered "macho" by her employer. Nevertheless, the Supreme Court's decision and reasoning in the case which undermined the reasoning of the *Holloway/Ulane* line of cases, expanded the potential legal protection of transgender persons under Title VII. Indeed, following the *Price Waterhouse* ruling, lower federal courts have relied on the Supreme Court's "sex-stereotyping" theory.

For example, in *Schwenk v. Hartford*, 204 F3d 1187 (9th Cir 2000), the Ninth Circuit held that "[t]he initial judicial approach in cases such as *Holloway* has been overruled by the logic and language of *Price Waterhouse*." The plaintiff in *Schwenk*, a transgender inmate in a Washington state prison, alleged that a prison guard subjected her to an unwelcome sexual attack in violation of the Gender Motivated Violence Act of 1994 (GMVA), an act which provides a cause of action for victims of gender-motivated violence. In analyzing whether the alleged crime was motivated by gender under the GMVA, the Ninth Circuit considered Title VII case law, stating that the GMVA "parallels Title VII." The court extended the *Price Waterhouse* theory that "[d]iscrimination because one fails to act in the way expected of a man or woman is forbidden under Title VII" to include protection for the transgender plaintiff; the perpetrator's action against her "stemmed from the fact that he believed [she] was a man who 'failed to act like' one."

Continuing the trend, the U.S. Court of Appeals for the Sixth Circuit in *Smith v. City of Salem*, 378 F3d 566 (6th Cir 2004), concluded that a transgender fire department employee had successfully asserted sex discrimination claims under Title VII because he alleged "that his failure to conform to sex stereotypes concerning how a man should look and behave was the driving force behind Defendants' actions." Jimmie Smith was born male but identified as a female. He alleged that when he began to express a more feminine appearance at work, coworkers commented that his appearance and mannerisms were not "masculine enough," and the fire department and various city officials initiated a plan to terminate him.

The district court dismissed the Title VII claims on the ground that plaintiff failed to state a claim for sex stereotyping pursuant to *Price Waterhouse*. The court reasoned that Mr. Smith merely "invoke[d] the term-of-art created by *Price Waterhouse*, that is, 'sex-stereotyping,'" and that his "real" claim was "based upon his transsexuality." On appeal, the Sixth Circuit held that Mr. Smith had in fact stated a claim of sex discrimination under Title VII. It found that the district court erred in relying on pre-*Price Waterhouse* cases that found "Congress had a narrow view of sex in mind" and "never considered nor intended that [Title VII] apply to anything other than the traditional concept of sex."

Gender Nonconformity Under Title VII

In *Smith*, the Sixth Circuit concluded: "After *Price Waterhouse*, an employer who discriminates against women because, for instance, they do not wear dresses or makeup, is engaging in sex discrimination because the discrimination would not occur but for the victim's sex. It follows that employers who discriminate against men because they do wear dresses and makeup, or otherwise act femininely, are also engaging in sex discrimination, because the discrimination would not occur but for the victim's sex." Moreover, the court clarified that *Price Waterhouse* did not make Title VII protection against sex stereotyping conditional or provide any reason to exclude Title VII coverage for "non-sex-stereotypical behavior" simply because the person is a transsexual. Thus, according to the Sixth Circuit, "[s]ex stereotyping based on a person's gender nonconforming behavior is impermissible discrimination, irrespective of the cause of that behavior; a label, such as 'transsexual,' is not fatal to a sex discrimination claim where the victim has suffered discrimination because of his or her gender non-conformity."

A number of federal district courts have also applied the sex-stereotyping theory to find protection for transgender persons under Title VII. For example, in *Tronetti v. TLC Healthnet Lakeshore Hospital*, No. 03-CV-0375E, 2003 WL 22757935 (WDNY Sept 26, 2003), the U.S. District Court for the Western District of New York held that a transgender plaintiff's Title VII claim against his employer, insomuch as it was based on alleged discrimination for failing to "act like a man," was actionable. Specifically, the plaintiff, a biological male who "assumed the social role of a woman" in terms of dress and appearance, claimed that his employer had advised him to avoid wearing overtly feminine attire, failed to investigate his complaint that he had become the subject of demeaning rumors concerning his sexuality and ultimately forced him to resign based on unfounded charges. Citing *Price Waterhouse* and *Schwenk*, the court rejected the employer's contention that the plaintiff's claims must fail because transsexuals are not protected under Title VII.

Despite the growing recognition of Title VII protection for transgender plaintiffs, post-*Price Waterhouse* courts have consistently held that Title VII does not prohibit discrimination based on sexual orientation. Indeed, the Second Circuit in *Dawson v. Bumble & Bumble*, 398 F3d 211 (2d Cir. 2005), stated that a Title VII sex-stereotype claim should not be used to "bootstrap" claims based on sexual orientation discrimination. The rationale is that such discrimination is based, not on sex, but on sexual orientation, and that discrimination based on sexual orientation is gender-neutral.

> "Smith *serves to enlarge the class of po-*
> *tential civil rights litigants by expand-*
> *ing coverage from relatively immutable*
> *personal characteristics to any type of*
> *behaviors a court finds nonstereotypi-*
> *cal.*"

Smith Expanded the Legal Understanding of Sex Discrimination Too Far

Paul E. Gugel

Paul E. Gugel is an attorney specializing in corporate and em-
ployment law and is general counsel for NeuroHealth, a mental
health organization.

In the following article, Gugel argues that the U.S. Court of
Appeals for the Sixth District went too far in Smith v. Salem,
Ohio, et al., *in finding that discrimination against transsexuals*
constitutes sex discrimination under Title VII of the Civil Rights
Act of 1964. Gugel claims that the plaintiff in Smith *suffered*
from gender identity disorder, a mental disorder according to the
American Psychiatric Association, and so should have filed a
case of disability discrimination. He contends that the case was
improperly decided under the theory of sex stereotyping because
gender identity disorder has not been granted civil rights protec-
tion by Congress. He concludes that the Smith *decision will re-*
sult in a flood of bogus discrimination cases.

Paul E. Gugel, "Of Fighting Fires and Firefighters: Sex Stereotyping in *Smith v. City of Salem*," *Michigan Bar Journal*, vol. 86, June 2007, pp. 34–36. Copyright © 2007, State Bar of Michigan. Reproduced by permission of the author.

The city of Salem, Ohio suspended one of its firefighters, [Jimmie L.] Smith, for a minor infraction. Smith, a transsexual, viewed the infraction as a pretext for sex discrimination and retaliation under Title VII of the Civil Rights Act of 1964. The trial court dismissed the suit on the grounds that Title VII protection is unavailable to transsexuals. On August 5, 2004, the Sixth Circuit Court of Appeals [in *Smith v. City of Salem*] reversed the decision on the theory of "sex stereotyping" sex discrimination.

Definition of Sex Stereotyping

The United States Supreme Court outlawed the practice of sex stereotyping in the landmark case of *Price Waterhouse v Hopkins* [1989]. Ms. Hopkins was a senior manager for a national public accounting firm. She was under consideration for promotion to partner—a process requiring review and approval by the existing partners, overwhelmingly male in number.

The partners voted against her promotion for two consecutive years, at which point she resigned and filed suit, alleging sex discrimination under Title VII. She claimed that she had been sex stereotyped by the partners, both supporters and detractors, who made comments implying that she was or had been acting masculine. A plurality of the Court stated that "an employer who acts on the basis of a belief that a woman cannot be aggressive, or that she must not be, has acted on the basis of gender." The Court concluded that such an action violated Title VII.

The Sixth Circuit

The *Smith* court, the Sixth Circuit Court of Appeals, has been understaffed since the [Bill] Clinton administration. There were four vacancies on the 16-member panel at the time *Smith* was argued.

The Sixth Circuit "has been declared a 'judicial emergency' by the Administrative Office of the U.S. Courts because of the length of the vacancies and the workload." As a result, the Sixth Circuit was the slowest appellate court to dispose of cases, taking an average of almost 17 months to do so in fiscal year 2003, compared to less than 11 months for the other 11 appellate courts. Given the vacancies and the caseload, judges from the other federal courts have been "on loan" to the Sixth Circuit. One of the judges sitting in the *Smith* case, the Honorable William W. Schwartzer, was a Senior United States District Judge for the Northern District of California. Not surprisingly, then, the *Smith* panel drew a significant amount of precedent from cases decided by the Ninth Circuit—the circuit court of appeals with jurisdiction over California. The Ninth Circuit is a circuit in which plaintiffs such as Smith have had more success with the argument that the *Hopkins* holding protects transvestites and transsexuals than plaintiffs in other circuits. For instance, in *Schwenk v Hartford* [9th Cir. 2000], the Ninth Circuit opined that "[d]iscrimination because one fails to act in the way expected of a man or woman is forbidden under Title VII."

A Disguised Disability Claim

The *Smith* decision noted early in its background section that the plaintiff suffered from gender identity disorder, a mental disorder recognized by the American Psychiatric Association. Why, then, did the plaintiff not file the case as a disability discrimination lawsuit under the Americans with Disabilities Act of 1990 (ADA)? Because the ADA specifically excludes transvestism and transsexualism from the definition of disabilities under that statute: "Under this Act, the term 'disability' shall not include—(1) transvestism, transsexualism, pedophilia, exhibitionism, voyeurism, gender identity disorders not resulting from physical impairments, or other sexual behavior disorders. . . ."

An equally intriguing question is, How did Smith's counsel and the Sixth Circuit convert an otherwise unrecognized disability claim into a cognizable Title VII sex discrimination claim? By extending the *Hopkins* sex-stereotyping argument to a plaintiff's behaviors, rather than a classification that Congress saw fit—in a 1990 statute passed *after* the 1989 *Hopkins* decision—to specifically exclude from the protections of the federal civil rights laws.

The lower court in *Smith* had concluded that "'Title VII does not prohibit discrimination based on an individual's transsexualism.'" The Sixth Circuit recharacterized the mental disorder as a choice of clothing and mannerisms:

> After *Price Waterhouse*, an employer who discriminates against women because, for instance, they do not wear dresses or makeup, is engaging in sex discrimination because the discrimination would not occur but for the victim's sex. It follows that employers who discriminate against men because they do wear dresses and makeup, or otherwise act femininely, are also engaging in sex discrimination, because the discrimination would not occur but for the victim's sex.

Some view the ADA as underinclusive because it specifically excludes certain mental disorders from the definition of disabilities and thereby deprives the sufferers of civil rights protection. But Congress—having added sex as a protected basis on which discrimination was prohibited under Title VII of the 1964 Civil Rights Act—specifically excluded transvestism and transsexualism from the ADA's coverage. The Sixth Circuit has made the ADA's mandated exclusion from civil rights protection for transvestites and transsexuals a nullity by minimizing (if not ignoring) the underlying mental disorders while simultaneously elevating their symptomatic behaviors to grounds for sex discrimination. Under the *Smith* rationale, there is no longer a need to exclude certain mental disorders from ADA civil rights coverage if those same disorders are reduced to mere sex/gender norms (i.e., behaviors) entitled to protection from *Hopkins* Title VII sex stereotyping. *Smith* thus overreached in defining sex discrimination and, in doing so, emasculated the ADA by granting civil rights protection to the transsexual plaintiff.

A Pandora's Box

This is not to say that transvestites and transsexuals should not be treated the same as other employees as long as they can perform their jobs adequately. But federal law does not yet require employers to do so, contrary to the Sixth Circuit's view in *Smith*.

In its effort to shoehorn the plaintiff into a classification protected by the Civil Rights Act, the *Smith* court opened the proverbial Pandora's Box for discrimination jurisprudence. No longer must successful plaintiffs be members of a protected class; all they must now show is behavior stereotypical to that class to qualify for protection as a member of that class. Smith wore women's clothes. The court said that his employer could not take action against him for his choice of feminine clothing. So, if a 50-something white male reports for work in dreadlocks and gold chains, speaking Ebonics [also called Black English], or if a white woman of Scandinavian descent shows up for work with her face almost completely covered by a veil, claiming religious freedom, the employer will not be able to base an adverse employment decision on the person's nonstereotypical behaviors. *Smith* suggests to employers that they cannot enforce a reasonable (read: stereotypical) code of conduct because to do so will unlawfully infringe on the individual's right to self-expression as a member of a protected class to which he or she does not belong, but merely aspires to belong—or chooses to mock. Employers cannot, however, concede to an ill-reasoned court decision. The best way to prohibit undesirable work behaviors is to draft an employee code of conduct reasonably, to train the workforce on it regularly, and to enforce it diligently.

Smith serves to enlarge the class of potential civil rights litigants by expanding coverage from relatively immutable personal characteristics to any type of behaviors a court finds nonstereotypical.

"By reiterating that discrimination
based on both sex and gender is forbidden under Title VII, the court steers
transgendered jurisprudence in a more
expansive and just direction."

Smith Rightfully Expanded the Legal Understanding of Sex Discrimination

Melinda Chow

Melinda Chow graduated from Harvard Law School in 2006
and is an attorney in New York.

In the following article, Chow argues that the decision by the
U.S. Court of Appeals for the Sixth District in Smith v. Salem,
Ohio, et al.—which found that discrimination based on gender
stereotypes toward transgendered people is prohibited by Title
VII of the Civil Rights Act—rightfully increased the legal protections of transgendered persons. Recounting the legal cases regarding claims of discrimination by transgendered persons prior to
Smith, Chow claims that the courts missed the real issue of gender discrimination. In Smith, she claims, the court accurately
sees discrimination against transgendered people based on gender stereotypes as an issue of sex discrimination prohibited under Title VII. She concludes that courts still have a way to go in
broadening their understanding of sex discrimination.

Melinda Chow, "*Smith v. City of Salem*: Transgendered Jurisprudence and an Expanding
Meaning of Sex Discrimination Under Title VII," *Harvard Journal of Law & Gender*, vol.
28, Winter 2005, pp. 207–15. Copyright © 2006 by the President and Fellows of Harvard
College. Reproduced by permission.

Transgendered people inhabit the outskirts of mainstream society. They have been marginalized, discriminated against, ridiculed, and even dehumanized. It is perhaps unsurprising, given this history of stigmatization, that transgendered people have not often found refuge in the law. In the context of sex discrimination, for example, courts have traditionally refused to expand protection against sex discrimination under Title VII of the Civil Rights Act to cover discrimination against transgendered people. Recently, however, some courts have become more amenable to protecting gender variants. These courts have built upon the Supreme Court's decision in *Price Waterhouse v. Hopkins* [1989], which granted Title VII relief to a woman who was discriminated against by her employer for being too "masculine," in order to provide antidiscrimination protection to transgendered plaintiffs. Other courts have refused to interpret the holding in *Price Waterhouse* as applying to transgendered people.

In light of this conflicting case law, it is significant that the Sixth Circuit recently took a strong stance on the expansion of transgendered rights. In *Smith v. City of Salem* [6th Cir. 2004], the court extended Title VII protection to a transsexual firefighter. The Sixth Circuit opinion is a welcome addition to antidiscrimination doctrine because transgendered people, so long marginalized by sex- and gender-based stereotypes, deserve legal protection. The reasoning in *Smith* is also significant because it expands the sex discrimination prohibited by Title VII to include discrimination based on both sex and gender.

A Groundbreaking Decision

Ulane v. Eastern Airlines, Inc. [7th Cir. 1984] was the leading case on transgendered employment discrimination prior to *Price Waterhouse* and the recent Ninth Circuit opinions. In *Ulane*, the Seventh Circuit denied Title VII sex discrimination protection to a transsexual pilot. The court narrowly interpreted sex discrimination as discrimination "against women because they are women and against men because they are men." The court further stated, "The words of Title VII do not outlaw discrimination against a person who has a sexual identity disorder." Justice [Antonin] Scalia, in order to keep gender out of the definition of "sex" discrimination, clarified in his dissent in a 1994 case the distinction between sex and gender: "The word 'gender' has acquired the new and useful connotation of cultural or attitudinal characteristics (as opposed to physical characteristics) distinctive to the sexes. That is to say, gender is to sex as feminine is to female and masculine is to male."

Five years after *Ulane*, in a groundbreaking case for gender jurisprudence, the Supreme Court held in *Price Waterhouse* that Title VII prohibits gender discrimination, which includes sex stereotyping. The court stated, "Title VII even forbids employers to make gender an indirect stumbling block to employment opportunities." In *Price Waterhouse*, the plaintiff, Ann Hopkins, was denied partnership at her accounting firm because she failed to conform to gender stereotypes of how women should look and act. Partners of the firm described her as "macho," noted that she "overcompensated for being a woman," recommended that she take "a course at charm school," and mentioned that she could improve her chances for partnership if she could "walk more femininely, talk more femininely, dress more femininely, have her hair styled, and wear jewelry." Following the *Price Waterhouse* precedent, the Ninth Circuit has also stated that Title VII "prohibit[s] discrimination based on gender as well as sex."

Sex as Biological Sex

Despite its groundbreaking holding, the potential impact of the *Price Waterhouse* decision has not been fully realized. In *Dobre v. National Railroad Passenger Corp.* [E.D. Pa. 1993], Amtrak hired the plaintiff, who "presented herself as a man," but who several months afterwards informed her supervisors that she was commencing hormone treatment for the process of becoming a biological female. In response, Amtrak required Dobre to dress as a male, forbade her to use the women's restroom, referred to her by her male name, and moved her desk away from public view. Like the courts in the pre–*Price Waterhouse* decisions, the *Dobre* court held that Title VII does not protect transsexuals from such discrimination because the term "sex" should be narrowly construed, according to its plain meaning, which it stated was biological and anatomical sex, a concept distinct from gender. In its opinion, the district court did not mention the *Price Waterhouse* case; instead it relied on the *Ulane* line of cases.

Even when courts have accepted the proposition that gender discrimination is included in the sex discrimination forbidden by Title VII and that Title VII prohibits sex stereotyping, they sometimes still deny protection to transgendered people by distinguishing Ann Hopkins's predicament in *Price Waterhouse* from more extreme forms of gender nonconformity. The courts that have taken this approach appear to believe [according to Sunish Gulati] that discrimination against transsexuals, transvestites, and transgendered people "is of a different and permissible sort." These courts insist that Title VII does not cover transsexuals because there is something categorically different between an effeminate male and a transgendered male that moves discrimination against transgendered males into the realm of permissible gender discrimination.

The plaintiff in *Oiler v. Winn-Dixie Louisiana, Inc.* [E.D. La. 2002] was a male cross-dresser diagnosed with transvestic fetishism and gender identity disorder ("GID") who was fired from his job at Winn-Dixie "because he publicly adopted a female persona and publicly cross-dressed as a woman." In an effort to distinguish Oiler's experience from Hopkins's in *Price Waterhouse*, the court clarified that this is not a situation where the plaintiff failed to a conform to a gender stereotype. . . . The plaintiff was terminated because he is a man with a sexual or gender identity disorder who, in order to publicly disguise himself as a woman, wears women's clothing, shoes, underwear, breast prostheses, wigs, make-up, and nail polish, pretends to be a woman, and publicly identifies himself as a woman.

The *Oiler* court assumed that the definition of gender stereotypes is not broad enough to include men with GID or men who dress like women. However, by definition, a gender stereotype is an assumption about how a person of a particular sex should look and act. For example, in *Price Waterhouse*, the gender stereotype was that women should wear jewelry and make-up. In *Oiler*, there was also a gender stereotype involved—that men should be gendered masculine and not wear make-up—and Oiler failed to conform to that stereotype. It is difficult for courts to overcome the stereotypical idea that men should want to appear masculine and women should want to appear feminine. Although *Price Waterhouse* outlawed discrimination based on this exact stereotype, gender nonconformists who pass beyond a certain degree of deviance are apparently too "unnatural" for some courts, like that in *Oiler*, to accept.

The Real Issue

In *James v. Ranch Mart Hardware* [D. Kan. 1995], the defendant hired Glenn Wayne James, biologically a male, for a sales clerk position. After James informed the store manager that she would become Barbara Renee James and wear a wig, a dress, and make-up in order to appear like a woman, the manager told James that he did not want her to come to work appearing in that manner, but agreed to discuss the idea with the president of Ranch Mart and to let James know the outcome. The manager spoke with the president, and the two decided to make a final decision the next day when James came to work, although they did not inform her of their conversation or decision. When James did not show up to work for the following two days, Ranch Mart fired her for her absence.

The district court held that James failed to state a claim of employment discrimination under Title VII. The court dismissed James's claim because she was not a member of a protected class as either a male or a transsexual and thus did not meet the first element of a prima facie [apparent] case of employment discrimination. In its discussion, the court explained that in order to evaluate James's claim, the court would have had to compare how James was treated, as a male, to the treatment of a similarly situated female, which the court determined was a female-to-male transsexual. The court should have compared James, a biological male who wore dresses, to a biological female who wore dresses and concluded that the female would not have been fired. Instead, the court said that it is permissible to discriminate against transsexuals as long as one discriminates against all transsexuals. The type of analysis suggested by the *James* court is a contrived method of avoiding the real issue of gender discrimination. It furthermore relies upon the assumption that discrimination against transsexuals and others who stray from gender-based stereotypes is acceptable.

The *Smith* Decision

Jimmie L. Smith was employed by the City of Salem (the "City") as a lieutenant in its fire department, where she worked without any negative incidents for seven years. Smith is a transsexual; she was born a biological male, but has a female sexual identity. After doctors diagnosed Smith with Gender Identity Disorder ("GID"), her co-workers began "commenting that [her] appearance and mannerisms were not 'masculine enough.'" Consequently, Smith spoke with her immediate supervisor, Thomas Eastek, about her GID diagnosis and treatment "so that Eastek could address Smith's co-workers' comments and inquiries." Shortly after, Eastek met with Walter

Greenamyer, the chief of the fire department, against Smith's wishes, and Greenamyer then discussed Smith's condition with the law director for the city, Brooke Zellers. "Greenamyer and Zellers arranged a meeting of the City's executive body to discuss Smith and devise a plan for terminating [her] employment." At the meeting, Zellers, Greenamyer, and the mayor of Salem agreed to have the City select physicians to conduct psychological evaluations of Smith on three separate occasions. "They hoped that Smith would either resign or refuse to comply" with these humiliating and scrutinizing requirements. Four days after Smith received a "right to sue" letter from the Equal Employment Opportunity Commission, Greenamyer suspended Smith for one twenty-four hour shift based on an alleged violation of an outdated policy.

As a result of these incidents, Smith filed Title VII claims of sex discrimination and retaliation, equal protection and due process claims under 42 U.S.C. [United States Code] § 1983, and state law claims of invasion of privacy and civil conspiracy. After determining that Title VII does not protect transsexuals as a class, the district court judge dismissed all of Smith's claims and granted summary judgment for the defendants on the federal claims.

On appeal, the Sixth Circuit first examined Smith's sex stereotyping claim in light of the Supreme Court's pronouncements in *Price Waterhouse*. The court found that Title VII's prohibition on discrimination because of sex bars gender discrimination. The court aptly observed that the district court relied on a series of pre–*Price Waterhouse* decisions that failed to include gender in the definition of "sex." According to the court, these decisions were "eviscerated" by the Supreme Court's logic in *Price Waterhouse*. From the Supreme Court's prohibition on discrimination against females who act too masculine, the Sixth Circuit extrapolated, "[i]t follows that employers who discriminate against men because they *do* wear dresses and makeup, or otherwise act femininely, are also engaging in sex discrimination, because the discrimination would not occur but for the victim's sex." The Sixth Circuit also further clarified the definition of "gender," which is a term "borrowed from grammar to designate the sexes as viewed as *social* rather than *biological* classes." Thus, the Sixth Circuit recognized that limiting the analysis of sex discrimination to biological categories is inadequate and thus expanded the bases upon which sex discrimination is forbidden.

Moreover, contrary to the *Oiler* and *James* courts, the Sixth Circuit held that Smith's status as a transsexual did not bar her claim. By definition, transsexuals are individuals who fail to conform to stereotypes about how those of a particular biological sex should act, dress, and self-identify. The Sixth Circuit clarified that from a legal perspective, a transsexual is not categorically different from a "macho" woman; the difference is only a matter of degree. Transsexuality is merely an extreme instance of a person whose biological sex fails to match his or her gender.

Second, the court held that Smith sufficiently pled that her suspension constituted an "adverse employment action." The court found that the fire department's suspension of Smith for a twenty-four-hour shift, which constituted 60% of a forty-hour workweek, was sufficient to establish a "materially adverse change in the terms and conditions of [plaintiff's] employment." On Smith's claims pursuant to 42 U.S.C. § 1983, the court held that Smith sufficiently stated a claim of sex discrimination in violation of her equal protection rights, but failed to state a claim based on violations of her right to due process. The court did not address the state law claims.

The Sixth Circuit correctly applied the *Price Waterhouse* decision to hold that transsexuals are protected against sex discrimination under Title VII. More broadly, the court clarified that the sex discrimination prohibited under Title VII includes gender-based discrimination. Thus, the Sixth Circuit increased the scope of protection available against sex discrimination by including multiple concepts of proscribed sex discrimination. This expansion is appropriate because sexual stereotypes and the discrimination that results from applying these stereotypes to the detriment of another often involves societal expectations of gender.

Further Progress on Gender Needed

The Sixth Circuit's holding and reasoning in *Smith* represents a significant victory for transgendered people. By reiterating that discrimination based on both sex and gender is forbidden under Title VII, the court steers transgendered jurisprudence in a more expansive and just direction. There are still other types of discrimination, however, that are currently not prohibited by Title VII, but that occur as a result of gender stereotyping.

To continue progress in this area, courts should extend Title VII protection to forbid discrimination based on sexual orientation and to prohibit gender-based dress codes. Courts have consistently denied Title VII protection to homosexuals on the basis that Title VII's use of the term "sex" does not include "sexual orientation." Like the *Oiler* and *Dobre* courts, which considered transsexuals categorically distinguishable from "sissy" men or "macho" women, courts denying protection to homosexuals also consider homosexuality a different and hence permissible basis for discrimination. Yet, like transsexuals, homosexuals can be seen as extreme gender nonconformers: they do not conform to the stereotype that men ought to desire women sexually or that women ought to desire men sexually. Homosexuality and transsexuality subvert norms and expectations about how women and men should live their lives as sexual beings. Traditional notions of sex and gender are transgressed by both homosexuals and transsexuals, but a progressive society must free itself from such outdated and rigid notions of human nature. Extending Title

VII protection to people discriminated against on the basis of sexual orientation is an important step toward achieving this goal.

Along the same lines, Title VII's prohibition on sex discrimination should also be interpreted to forbid gender-based dress codes. Such dress codes have been upheld on the grounds that grooming policies are "not within the statutory goal of equal employment" and because the policies supposedly only have a "de minimis [minimal] effect." The Seventh Circuit has stated, "So long as [dress codes] find some justification in commonly accepted social norms and are reasonably related to the employer's business needs, such regulations are not necessarily violations of Title VII even though the standards prescribed differ somewhat for men and women." This type of stereotype-accommodating attitude only undermines the goal of equality. Norms about clothing, grooming, hair, and physical appearance in general often originate from gender stereotypes. Thus, dress codes that force people to dress in ways expected of those of their biological sex are mechanisms that reinforce gender stereotypes and create backlash against gender nonconformists. Courts that uphold these dress codes are therefore sanctioning gender discrimination.

The obstacles to expanding Title VII to forbid discrimination against homosexuals and to outlaw gender-based dress codes are not insurmountable. Before *Price Waterhouse*, the outlook for transsexuals seemed grim. The Sixth Circuit's holding in *Smith* demonstrates that courts can successfully transcend deeply ingrained societal prejudices and decide cases based on sound legal principles that accurately reflect the complexities involved with sex and gender.

Organizations to Contact

The editors have compiled the following list of organizations concerned with the issues debated in this book. The descriptions are derived from materials provided by the organizations. All have publications or information available for interested readers. The list was compiled on the date of publication of the present volume; the information provided here may change. Be aware that many organizations take several weeks or longer to respond to inquiries, so allow as much time as possible.

American Civil Liberties Union (ACLU)
125 Broad St., 18th Fl., New York, NY   10004
(212) 549-2500
e-mail: infoaclu@aclu.org
Web site: www.aclu.org

The American Civil Liberties Union (ACLU) is a national organization that seeks to defend the rights guaranteed by the U.S. Constitution. Its primary work is to support court cases against government actions that violate these rights. The ACLU publishes and distributes numerous policy statements and reports, including "Venus and Mars in Separate Classrooms?"

Cato Institute
1000 Massachusetts Ave. NW, Washington, DC   20001-5403
(202) 842-0200 • fax: (202) 842-3490
Web site: www.cato.org

The Cato Institute is a public policy research foundation dedicated to limiting the role of government, protecting individual liberties, and promoting free markets. The institute commissions a variety of publications, including books, monographs, briefing papers and other studies. Among its publications are the quarterly magazine *Regulation* and the bimonthly *Cato Policy Report*.

Concerned Women for America (CWA)

1015 Fifteenth St. NW, Ste. 1100, Washington, DC   20005
(202) 488-7000 • fax: (202) 488-0806
Web site: www.cwfa.org

Concerned Women for America (CWA) is a public policy women's organization that has the goal of bringing biblical principles into all levels of public policy making. CWA promotes biblical values on six core issues—family, sanctity of human life, education, pornography, religious liberty, and national sovereignty—through prayer, education, and social influence. Among the organization's brochures, fact sheets, and articles available on its Web site is "Entitled to Emasculate."

Equal Rights Advocates (ERA)

1663 Mission St., Ste. 250, San Francisco, CA   94103
(415) 621-0672 • fax: (415) 621-6744
e-mail: info@equalrights.org
Web site: www.equalrights.org

Equal Rights Advocates (ERA) works to protect and secure equal rights and economic opportunities for women and girls. It fights for women's equality through litigation and advocacy. ERA produces several publications covering issues of equal opportunity, respectful and safe treatment, and work and family balance, including the Know Your Rights series brochure titled *Sex Discrimination.*

Human Rights Campaign (HRC)

1640 Rhode Island Ave. NW, Washington, DC   20036-3278
(202) 628-4160 • fax: (202) 347-5323
e-mail: hrc@hrc.org
Web site: www.hrc.org

The Human Rights Campaign (HRC) is America's largest civil rights organization working to achieve gay, lesbian, bisexual, and transgender (GLBT) equality. HRC works to secure equal rights for GLBT individuals at the federal and state levels by lobbying elected officials and mobilizing grassroots supporters. Among the organization's publications is the report "Transgender Inclusion in the Workplace."

Lambda Legal

120 Wall St., Ste. 1500, New York, NY   10005-3904
(212) 809-8585 • fax: (212) 809-0055
e-mail: members@lambdalegal.org
Web site: www.lambdalegal.org

Lambda Legal is a legal organization working for the civil rights of lesbians, gay men, and people with HIV/AIDS. The organization works toward this goal by pursuing impact litigation, education, and advocacy to make the case for equality in state and federal court, the Supreme Court, and in the court of public opinion. Among the many publications the organizations produces is the article "Transgender Rights."

Leadership Conference on Civil Rights (LCCR)

1629 K St. NW, 10th Fl., Washington, DC   20006
(202) 466-3311
Web site: www.civilrights.org

Leadership Conference on Civil Rights (LCCR) is a coalition of over 190 national human rights organizations. Its mission is to promote the enactment and enforcement of effective civil rights legislation and policy. There are numerous fact sheets and other publications available at LCCR's Web site, including "Key Supreme Court Cases for Civil Rights."

Legal Momentum

395 Hudson St., New York, NY   10014
(212) 925-6635 • fax: (212) 226-1066
e-mail: policy@legalmomentum.org
Web site: www.legalmomentum.org

Legal Momentum is the nation's oldest legal defense and education fund dedicated to advancing the rights of all women and girls. Legal Momentum works to advance these rights through litigation and public policy advocacy to secure economic and personal security for women. Among the publications available from Legal Momentum is the report "From the Ground Up: Building Opportunities for Women in Construction."

National Coalition for Men (NCFM)
932 C St., Ste. B, San Diego, CA 92101
(619) 231-1909
e-mail: ncfm@ncfm.org
Web site: www.ncfm.org

The National Coalition for Men (NCFM) is a nonprofit educational organization committed to ending sex discrimination. NCFM works to raise awareness about the ways sex discrimination affects men and boys. Among the publications available at NCFM's Web site is the article "Men's Reproductive Rights."

National Organization for Women (NOW)
1100 H St. NW, 3rd Fl., Washington, DC 20005
(202) 628-8669 • fax: (202) 785-8576
Web site: www.now.org

National Organization for Women (NOW) is the largest organization of feminist activists in the United States taking action to bring about equality for all women. NOW works to eliminate discrimination and harassment in the workplace, schools, the justice system, and all other sectors of society; to secure abortion, birth control and reproductive rights for all women; to end all forms of violence against women; to eradicate racism, sexism and homophobia; and to promote equality and justice in our society. NOW has many publications available on its Web site, including the fact sheet "Women Deserve Equal Pay."

For Further Research

Books

Howard Ball, *The Supreme Court in the Intimate Lives of Americans: Birth, Sex, Marriage, Childrearing, and Death*. New York: New York University Press, 2002.

Katherine T. Bartlett, *Gender and Law: Theory, Doctrine, Commentary*. 5th ed. New York: Aspen, 2009.

Barbara J. Berg, *Sexism in America: Alive, Well, and Ruining Our Future*. Chicago: Lawrence Hill Books, 2009.

Barry Friedman, *The Will of the People: How Public Opinion Has Influenced the Supreme Court and Shaped the Meaning of the Constitution*. New York: Farrar, Straus, and Giroux, 2009.

David J. Garrow, *Liberty and Sexuality: The Right to Privacy and the Making of* Roe v. Wade. New York: Macmillan, 1994.

Linda C. McClain and Joanna L. Grossman, eds., *Gender Equality: Dimensions of Women's Equal Citizenship*. New York: Cambridge University Press, 2009.

Sandra Day O'Connor, *The Majesty of the Law: Reflections of a Supreme Court Justice*. New York: Random House, 2003.

Gerald N. Rosenberg, *The Hollow Hope: Can Courts Bring About Social Change?* Chicago: University of Chicago Press, 2008.

Jay Sekulow, *Witnessing Their Faith: Religious Influence on Supreme Court Justices*. Lanham, MD: Rowman & Littlefield, 2006.

Melvin I. Urofsky, *Affirmative Action on Trial: Sex Discrimination in* Johnson v. Santa Clara. Lawrence: University Press of Kansas, 1997.

Lee Walzer, *Marriage on Trial: A Handbook with Cases, Laws, and Documents.* Santa Barbara, CA: ABC-CLIO, 2005.

Joan Williams, *Unbending Gender: Why Family and Work Conflict and What to Do About It.* New York: Oxford University Press, 2000.

Periodicals

Rostker v. Goldberg (1981)

Mario L. Barnes, "'But Some of (Them) Are Brave': Identity Performance, the Military, and the Dangers of an Integration Success Story," *Duke Journal of Gender Law & Policy*, May 2007.

Chris Branstad, "Equal Rights Means Drafting Women, Too," *Iowa State Daily*, November 14, 2007.

Martha F. Davis, "The Equal Rights Amendment: Then and Now," *Columbia Journal of Gender and Law*, Fall 2008.

Elaine Donnelly, "Constructing the Co-ed Military," *Duke Journal of Gender Law & Policy*, May 2007.

Jill Elaine Hasday, "Fighting Women: The Military, Sex, and Extrajudicial Constitutional Change," *Minnesota Law Review*, November 2008.

Maggie Koerth, "Women in Draft Necessary Part of Quest to End Discrimination," *University Daily Kansan*, February 5, 2003.

Diane H. Mazur, "Military Values in Law," *Duke Journal of Gender Law & Policy*, May 2007.

Martha McSally, "Women in Combat: Is the Current Policy Obsolete?" *Duke Journal of Gender Law & Policy*, May 2007.

Carol Judith Ormond, "G.I. Joe: *Rostker* and Women in the Military—A Setback in Advancing Equal Protection Analysis?" *Beverly Hills Bar Association Journal*, Summer 1985.

Ilya Somin, "Be Careful What You Wish For," *Legal Times*, June 4, 2007.

Price Waterhouse v. Hopkins (1989)

Daniel A. Farber, "Proving Discrimination in Title VII Cases," *Trial*, August 1989.

Joel William Friedman, "Gender Nonconformity and the Unfulfilled Promise of *Price Waterhouse v. Hopkins*," *Duke Journal of Gender Law & Policy*, January 2007.

Ann Hopkins, *"Price Waterhouse v. Hopkins*: A Personal Account of a Sexual Discrimination Plaintiff," *Hofstra Labor & Employment Law Journal*, Spring 2005.

Tony Mauro, "Court Remains Befuddled by Title VII," *Legal Times*, May 15, 1989.

Carolyn M. Plump, "Some Anti-gay Bias Is Already Against the Law," *National Law Journal*, October 1, 2007.

N. Thompson Powers, "Is *Price Waterhouse* a Help to Victims of Sex Discrimination?" *Legal Times*, May 15, 1989.

Michael Starr and Adam J. Heft, "Appearance Bias," *National Law Journal*, June 20, 2005.

Michael Starr and Amy L. Strauss, "Sex Stereotyping in Employment: Can the Center Hold?" *Labor Lawyer*, Winter 2006.

Mary Kathryn Zachary, "Labor Law," *Supervision*, June 2007.

United States v. Virginia (1996)

Margo L. Ely, "Court's VMI Decision Reinforces Review Standard for Sex Bias," *Chicago Daily Law Bulletin*, July 8, 1996.

Garrett Epps, "A Matter of Interpretation: Federal Courts and the Law," *Nation*, January 27, 1997.

Ann Farmer, "The Personal Is Still Political," *Perspectives*, Summer 2008.

Steven Frias, "Flagrant Disregard for Tradition: The Demise of Single Sex Education," *Suffolk University Law Review*, Winter 1997.

Katie Gibson, "*United States v. Virginia*: A Rhetorical Battle Between Progress and Preservation," *Women's Studies in Communication*, Fall 2006.

Marcia D. Greenberger and Deborah L. Brake, "The VMI Decision: Shattering Sexual Stereotypes," *Chronicle of Higher Education*, July 5, 1996.

Susan Reiger, "VMI and the Old/New Face of Sex Discrimination," *Federal Lawyer*, October 1996.

Kevin M. Rolando, "A Decade Later: *United States v. Virginia* and the Rise and Fall of 'Skeptical Scrutiny,'" *Roger Williams University Law Review*, Fall 2006.

Sharon Elizabeth Rush, "Diversity: The Red Herring of Equal Protection," *American University Journal of Gender and the Law*, Fall 1997.

Kathleen M. Sullivan, "Decisions Expand Equal Protection Rights," *National Law Journal*, July 29, 1996.

Elizabeth Weil, "Teaching to Testosterone," *New York Times Magazine*, March 2, 2008.

Smith v. Salem, Ohio, et al. (2004)

John Cloud, "A Transsexual vs. the Government," *Time*, September 12, 2008.

Anna Kirkland, "What's at Stake in Transgender Discrimination as Sex Discrimination?" *Signs*, Autumn 2006.

Brian P. McCarthy, "Trans Employees and Personal Appearance Standards Under Title VII," *Arizona Law Review*, Fall 2008.

James G. O'Keefe, "Pyrrhic Victory: *Smith v. City of Salem* and the Title VII Rights of Transsexuals," *DePaul Law Review*, Spring 2007.

Correy E. Stephenson, "Cases Involving Transgender Clients Becoming Increasingly Common," *Lawyers Weekly USA*, September 12, 2005.

Cole Thaler, "Transforming a Body of Law," *Of Counsel*, May 24, 2007.

Kenneth M. York, Catherine L. Tyler, J. Michael Tyler, and Paul E. Gugel, "The Ever-Changing Face of Sex Stereotyping and Sex Discrimination in the Workplace," *Journal of Leadership & Organizational Studies*, November 2008.

Index